I've Been Thinking...

...about Living, Loving, and Learning

Carol Goodman Heizer

Alpha Publishing
a division of Alpha Consulting
Louisville, KY

Alpha Publishing
A division of Alpha Consulting

First Edition, March, 1997
Copyright © 1997 by Carol Goodman Heizer

ISBN 0-9656402-1-3
Printed in U.S.A.
Louisville, KY

Library of Congress Catalog Card Number: 96-95412

For information about books, tapes, and seminars,
contact:
Alpha Publishing
A division of Alpha Consulting
P.O. Box 18433
Louisville, KY 40261-0433
Phone (502) 239-0761
FAX (502) 239-0764

Cover photo by Carol G. Heizer

DEDICATED to

YESTERDAY's thinkers who accomplished things
others thought impossible.

TODAY's thinkers who are learning from the great
minds of the past, yet continue to make their
own footprints in the sands of thought.

TOMORROW's thinkers who will broaden and enrich
our world in ways we cannot imagine.

Contents

Foreword

How many times in the midst of our daily lives have we found ourselves "just thinking"? Thinking about ourselves and others? Thinking about our loved ones, friends, and acquaintances, and our relationships to them? Thinking about life and the world in general? Thinking about why things happen as they do? Thinking about those things that have happened to *us* and the lessons we have learned, or perhaps failed to learn, from them?

How often have we asked ourselves who are we really, why are we here, what is our purpose, what is life all about, where do we "fit in" in the overall scheme of things, where are we going with our lives and are we taking the right road, and on and on?

If we are honest with ourselves, we must confess that the longer we live, the more frequently these thoughts just seem to pop into our minds — usually during our quiet reflective moments but at other times during the hustle and bustle of everyday living when we find ourselves coming to an abrupt halt for one reason or another.

Like us, Carol Heizer has also found herself "just thinking." But luckily for us she has done something that most of us never do. She has put her thoughts on paper so that she might share them with us, her readers. In turn, it is my belief that this will encourage each of us to *think even more*. And, hopefully, we will have the good fortune and life-enriching experience of not just keeping our thoughts to ourselves but of sharing them *and* ourselves with one another. What a wonderful opportunity for *all* of us to keep on *growing* every day of our lives!

Bob Wade, Ed.D
President
Wade & Associates
Louisville, Kentucky

. . . about

HOME

"He is happiest, be he king or peasant,
who finds peace in his home."

- Goethe

She Didn't!

Part I

I don't remember a lot about middle school. Perhaps it was because life was too hectic to remember much. Perhaps because life was so traumatic at that age, I do not *want* to remember much. Or perhaps it is because life was so boring at that point in time, there *is* not much to remember.

But one thing I do remember! I remember having a bad habit. My mother had discussed it with me on several occasions. She had asked me to stop doing it. She had begged me. She had threatened me. But nothing seemed to help. I didn't mean to disobey. I didn't mean to make her life miserable. It just seemed to keep happening . . . again and again.

I had plenty of closet space in my bedroom. I had plenty of drawer space. But my clothes didn't end up in either place. They kept *appearing* under my bed. I can remember my reasoning. If they were already dirty, what difference did it make if I shoved them under the bed? If they were *not* dirty and could, perhaps, be worn again, putting them under the bed kept me from having to properly put them away. After all, Mama knew where I kept my clothes. And she would get them before doing the laundry.

I was beginning to think I was one smart cookie!

She hadn't said anything for a long time, so I was feeling pretty comfortable in thinking I had won this small battle. She was probably getting pretty tired of harassing me about my clothes under the bed and had most likely decided to just give up and keep dragging them out on laundry day.

Boy, was I wrong! Did she have a surprise in store for me! And it was a memorable one. One that I am remembering 40 years later!

Actually, I wasn't *completely* wrong. My mother **was** getting pretty tired of harassing me about putting my clothes away. About that, I was correct. But from that point on, my mother and I were on different wave lengths, and *my* wave length was about to get a knot yanked in it.

It was late afternoon, and I arrived home after having survived another day in the educational institution known by society as *school*. They told me I was learning something and should be thankful for the opportunity. The only opportunity I was thankful for was to be home for the rest of the day. With my school books dropped in their usual corner, I headed for my room to change into play clothes. Except for the little bit of homework I had, the remainder of the day was mine. To explore. To imagine. To create. To waste. Whatever! It was mine!

I followed the usual procedure without even thinking about it. Off came the shoes, the skirt, the blouse, and the slip. *Kids back then didn't wear the kinds of clothes to school they wear today! We had to clean up and look decent!*

I grabbed my play clothes from one of my drawers, bent over, and proceeded to shove my clothes . . . where else . . . under the bed. As I was raising up, my eye caught something unusual on the front of my closet. I didn't recognize the object at first. I took another look.

What???!!!

She couldn't!!!

She wouldn't!!!

She did!!!

She had really done it!!!

There . . . on the front of my closet . . . as big as life itself . . . was the brightest, shiniest **padlock** I had ever seen!

I didn't need to ask *who* did it.

I knew.

I didn't need to ask *why* she did it.

I knew that, too.

Thunderbolt number ONE had just struck!

I was shocked beyond words. I could hardly believe my eyes. My ears were ringing, my hands were sweating, my heart was pounding, and my breathing was rapid. I was going to have a heart attack in my own bedroom! And I was only in the 8th grade! Eighth graders didn't have heart attacks! But I was about to have one! How would my parents explain my death? What would the neighbors say?

All this from the woman who always said she loved me. All this from the woman I thought had gotten pretty tired of harassing me and had decided to give up.

I thought of pounding my fist in anger.

I thought of screaming bloody murder.

I thought of running away and joining the circus.

I thought of demanding an explanation.

None of these options seemed too wise.

I thought of committing my mother to a mental institution. That didn't seem too wise either. No one would listen to me. I was only an eighth grader.

I went racing out of my bedroom, down the stairs, into the living room where my mother was lying on the sofa, and frantically and angrily asked, "What am I supposed to wear to school tomorrow?" (This was only Tuesday.)

She looked at me with the most peaceful expression and quietly said, "Wear what's under your bed."

What was under my bed! Those clothes were dirty! They were

wrinkled! That would mean I had to launder them! I thought of begging. I thought of pleading. I thought of pitching a royal fit.

Then I thought of doing the wisest thing possible . . . keep my mouth shut, gather my mound of clothes from under my bed, head for the basement, and launder them. I knew that when she saw me headed to the basement, she would realize I had learned my lesson, tell me she would follow through with the discipline the next time, and then tell me to put my clothes in the laundry hamper.

After my ears stopped ringing, my hands stopped sweating, and my heart stopped pounding, I gathered my clothes and headed toward the first floor on my way to the basement. I knew my mother was still lying on the sofa and that she would see me as I reached the bottom of the steps. I made up my mind that she would not get the best of me. Although I *knew* this constituted child abuse, I would behave in a mature manner. After all, I *had* been warned. Lots of times. So I guess I deserved this shock. It had worked. But it was about over. Now, if I could just control myself.

Wrong again!

As I reached the first floor, my mother looked at me with the most deadpan expression I have ever seen and calmly asked, "Where are you going?"

I remember thinking to myself . . . *Where do you **think** I'm going? To the grocery store?* But I remained firm in my resolve to behave in a mature manner. I remember looking at Mama and saying in the calmest tone I could muster, "I'm going to the basement to launder these clothes."

P.S. I know you're probably laughing right now. Especially if you're a mother. But I assure you . . . it wasn't the least bit funny to me then.

She Didn't!
Part II

I waited.

And I waited.

What was she waiting for? Why didn't she just go ahead and give me the little sermon about learning my lesson, not doing it again, and putting my clothes in the laundry hamper?

She simply looked at me with that *mother* expression again and said, "No, you're not. You're going to wear them just like they are. No laundering."

Thunderbolt number TWO had just struck!

I vaguely remember screaming, "WWWhhhaaattt! What do you mean, 'Wear them like they are'? I can't wear them like they are! They're dirty, and they're wrinkled!"

All she did was quietly reply, "They wouldn't be if you had put them away properly."

This woman had gone mad.

She had totally lost her marbles.

I was so angry I could hardly talk. But I finally gained enough composure to say in a civilized tone (I think), "Well, at least I can iron them" and started to walk away.

I should have known better.

In that calm voice which I had begun to hate within the last five minutes, she informed me, "No, you will not iron them either."

Thunderbolt number THREE had just struck!

How many thunderbolts did "Mother Nature" have?

I was trying to survive in the midst of a natural disaster! And I wasn't doing such a hot job of it, either! I truly cannot remember the remainder of that conversation. I think the shock was so intense, I have erased it from my memory.

I *do* remember not sleeping well that night. I also remember deciding to do *anything* to keep from going to school the following day. I would look like something that crawled out of a rag bag. And I was not about to humiliate myself like that!

I had a plan.

I got out of bed when called, as usual, the next morning. I had to play this thing right if it was going to work. I didn't do anything that would be too obvious. But I deliberately moved slowly and kept that *oh, I don't feel good* look on my face. I didn't say anything. I wanted **her** to notice it first. Finally, when it was obvious she wasn't going to notice, I quietly said, "I don't feel good." Nothing dramatic . . . just enough to raise suspicion.

I knew my mother was cruel, insensitive, and crazy by this point. But she wasn't vicious. She wouldn't send me to school if she thought I was truly sick.

My big break came when she said, "Go get the thermometer and put it in your mouth. Let's see."

Finally, things were going my way. I went upstairs, got that little sucker out of its container, and decided to make *sure* I had a fever. The water coming from the faucet was steaming hot, and I held that "fever meter" under the water for what I considered to be a sufficient amount of time. After all, I had to make sure *something* registered.

I put that thermometer in my mouth, went downstairs immediately, and dejectedly handed the thing to my mother. I tried to look as sick as possible.

I sure wished I could read a thermometer!

Mama looked at that thermometer for the longest time. I could almost read her thoughts. I *knew* she was thinking she had so traumatized me that she had literally made me ill. I *knew* she was feeling intense guilt. I *knew* I was going to be home for the day. At least I had escaped *one* day of wearing those horrible looking clothes.

She looked at the thermometer. Then at me. Then at the ther-mometer. Then at me . . . again. Wow, I had really done a good job! I had finally pulled one over on her. I was just about ready to tell myself, "Good job, kid. You finally did it," when she seemed to stare a hole through me . . . and calmly said, "Well, you don't look too bad for someone who has a temperature of 106 degrees."

LIGHTNING HAD JUST EXPLODED UPON THE EARTH, AND I HAD BEEN ITS PRIME TARGET!

I guess it's pretty hard to fool a registered nurse. I had forgot-ten about that. Why couldn't I have a regular mother like every-one else? Why did my mother have to be a *nurse*?

I spent the next three days at school trying to avoid everyone. I felt like something that had slithered out from under a rock. I prayed for the school floor to open up and swallow me. I prayed for a raging flood. I prayed for broken water pipes at school. I prayed that an outbreak of the plague would suddenly descend upon society. I prayed for *anything* to end my misery.

But nothing did.

For three days, I endured the agony of wearing dirty, rumpled, wrinkled, rag-a-muffin-looking outfits. I must give my mother credit for one speck of humanity through all of this. She was a health and hygiene freak, so I *was* permitted to have clean under-wear. But in spite of that consideration, death would have been a welcome visitor.

Only years later did I learn that my mother had called the school principal, told him of my "learning experience," and asked him to please cooperate in her lesson. Then I understood why I had had the misfortune of running into that man for three straight days and having him ask me every day, "Hi, Carol. How are you today?"

That was the only time in my three years at that school I had encountered the principal for three days straight running. And I thought it had been coincidence!

I learned several valuable lessons during that "padlock on the closet" episode.

I learned not to hold thermometers under hot water.

I learned to listen when my mother would repeat a warning . . . about anything.

I learned not to underestimate my mother's intelligence.

I learned not to underestimate my mother's strong will.

And I learned not to play stupid mind games with my mother.

For when I did, I lost!

She didn't!

And today . . . forty years after the fact, and a mother myself . . . I realize the courage and determination that my mother possessed. It took a strong, caring parent to commit herself to such extreme measures. But Mama was more concerned that her daughter learn a valuable lesson than whether that daughter would be angry with her mother for a period of time.

I Do! Do I?

I have recently been taking a long look at my marriage of almost 30 years. I have also been looking at a lot of other marriages, both of newlyweds and long-timers. Several interesting observations have emerged, but one question in particular keeps arising as I watch the relationship of married partners.

How can a husband and wife who are in love and married, who supposedly live the most intimate life possible, *not* discuss areas of conflict as they arise within the marital relationship?

At first I thought it was a fluke. But then, as I watched a lot of couples, I decided it was a consistent pattern. Individuals who appear to be free and open in their relationships with friends and acquaintances oftentimes seem to find it very difficult to be equally free and open in expressing themselves to their spouse. Why?

Perhaps it is because the individual, due to the intimacy of the marital bond, feels most vulnerable and fears self-disclosure. Or perhaps it is the uncertainty of a position upon the particular issue, and the individual is afraid of being questioned as to his or her reasons. Of course, either of these reasons would most likely be rooted in childhood "sharing experiences" that resulted in unpleasant and painful memories.

Think back to your childhood days when you were learning to form relationships. You talked to someone about something that was bothering you. Perhaps you were feeling fearful, or guilty, or anxious concerning something you were experiencing. The very person in whom you had confided, with whom you had shared your innermost self, either made you feel guilty, told you not to be so silly, made light of your situation, or even laughed at you. Or perhaps this person did not respect your privacy, and you later learned that your confidant shared your conversation with someone else.

Remember the betrayal you felt?

And what was the message you received from their response? *In order to be safe, keep it to yourself.*

Right? It was a message you received loud and clear! It was a lesson learned early . . . and learned well.

Time passed, but not the memory of your experience. If this scenario was repeated throughout your childhood, the image became so deeply cut into your heart that you carried the hurt into your adult relationships. Even into your marriage.

The bitter irony of this failure to discuss matters is that your spouse is one of the most significant persons in the world to whom you should look for encouragement and support and affirmation. Yet that most significant person in your life is often the one from whom you recoil the most.

We have always heard that "opposites attract" within a relationship, and money management is often another area of conflict. Concerning money, it is frequently the case that one partner is an extravagant spender, while the spouse is the typical scrooge. The interesting aspect of such a situation is that either spouse may have come from a home life that was typical of his or her personal spending habits. Perhaps he or she may have come from a background of opposite money management.

For instance, the scrooge learned stingy spending at an early age observing parents who counted every penny before spending it. On the opposite end of the scale, the scrooge (having observed such spending habits), may resort to the opposite extreme and find it difficult to save any money . . . wanting to spend as much money as possible as quickly as possible. If we were to conduct a study of this question, I wonder which direction the majority of respondents would tend to go?

Showing outward affection is another area in which there seems to be a great deal of stress among married couples. It could almost be said that there is not *one* marriage involved, but *two* . . . **his** version of what the marriage should be, and **her** version. And somewhere along the line, the two of them create a *third* marriage which is neither of their ideas, or a bad compromise of the two versions.

Women view open affection as a reminder of committed love, whereas many men tend to view it as either unnecessary or an indicator of a more intensely physical action that is about to take place. As a result, many women feel taken for granted on a daily basis.

Men are often genuinely surprised when confronted with the female's view, and their usual response is, "Well, you know I love you." This means that their love is shown through the provision of home, food, and other tangible assets.

Yet this thinking raises an interesting question. If this is the true male perspective, why did they go to such lengths to show outward affection and consideration during the courtship? Such courtship habits would obviously point to the fact that, somewhere in their male make-up, there was an awareness of the need for open affection. But before any undue blame is placed upon the male, we (as women) must ask ourselves if our behavior has changed in a manner that would make our spouse's behavior change.

The male response to this calamity, in addition to his assumption that the wife knows he loves her, is the position that he has become wrapped up in his work and his husbandly and fatherly responsibilities. This is frequently countered by the wife's argument that she, too, has great demands placed upon her.

Thus, it would appear to be obviously simple for the husband and wife to merely sit down and share their own wants and needs within the relationship in a calm and relaxed manner and place.

But there seems to be an inborn sense of martyrdom in many marriages. Thousands of spouses yearly continue through life, suffering in silence for the sake of the children (among other reasons), wanting the partner to supply that which he or she does not even realize the loved one needs.

A classic case of *same house, separate lives.*

But we are reasoning, adult human beings. We have the freedom of choice. If we find ourselves in this situation, do we want that situation to continue as it is? If so, then do nothing! But if we have somehow fallen into this *"I want something, and you're not giving it to me"* pattern, and we want the situation to change . . . we **can** do something about it.

Do we love that special someone in our life enough to sit down with him or her and attempt to correct the situation? Do we realize that such a conversation will most likely be difficult and perhaps frustrating at times? Are we willing to work our way around this stumbling block? Or do we simply decide to give up and live with the situation as it is?

If we have already attempted to discuss the matter and have seen no success, then what? Do we run up the white flag of surrender, or do we give it another shot? Isn't it worth another attempt? Isn't it worth trying to work around this difficulty in hopes of bettering our relationship with the person we love?

Relationships that are worth anything cannot be bought. They cannot be started and then taken for granted. They cannot be ignored. Relationships must be embarked upon, nourished, cultivated, and protected.

Relationships are like flowers. Many may be grouped into a

class of similar characteristics, but each one is uniquely different. No two are exactly the same. Each has its own requirements, not only for mere survival but for flourishing as well. Relationships, like flowers, must be properly cared for, or they will perish. And problems, like weeds, will take over if not constantly treated or removed.

When he was five or six years old, my son Mark once asked me, "Mom, why do you have to take care of the flowers, but the weeds grow all by themselves?" Quite an insightful question from a little guy, I'd say!

But remember this — "Out of the mouths of babes . . . ."

I don't remember my response to Mark, but I vividly recall my astonishment that such a little fellow could ask such a profound question containing such deep, far-reaching implications.

Why *do* weeds grow all by themselves? Because, like all problems, they multiply simply by being left alone.

And why *do* we have to take care of the flowers?

Because, like all fruitful endeavors, they thrive and enrich our lives by receiving the care and attention they need.

That's just the way it is!

You're Not the Person I Married

I've been thinking about this institution called *marriage*. I've been wondering how husbands and wives are expected to live together in peace and harmony, especially when the apparent basic principle of dating and marriage is that opposites fascinate and attract?

Several experts state that opposites attract due to the fact that they are searching for the "shadow" of themselves, attempting to join with another person who exhibits those qualities or tendencies which are underdeveloped or missing within themselves.

Initially, this explanation sounds reasonable and complete. Yet upon further consideration, one realizes that the answer itself raises other questions. For instance, if one is attracted to a person of the opposite nature, why is it the tendency of that first person to try and *change* the second person after marriage? Second, since so many people are consciously aware of many of their tendencies, what is it within individuals that realizes their true nature and looks for an opposite nature which serves as a complement?

Is this mate-choosing a conscious choice, or is it a deeper subconscious choice?

I have been reading various opinions lately that partially answer the first question concerning the attempt to change one's mate. The explanation is that it is the desire to *recast* oneself in an effort to *transform* the raw material of the mate. Yet that gives rise to the question that if we want to transform our mate's nature, was our appreciation of our mate's opposite nature the *only* factor that initially fascinated us? If so, why are we attempting to change that which attracted us? Would not logical reasoning lead us to the conclusion that we would be eliminating that which we wanted?

Pertaining to the second question of one's nature . . . if we are often unaware of our own basic self, yet we are competent to choose an *opposite*, at what level are we humanly able to function in carrying out this task? Is it not possible for the human mind to be so complicatedly constructed that no amount of medical or psychological expertise can truly comprehend it?

It is my firm belief that individuals try to change their mates for two basic reasons. First, most persons want to control things, people, and circumstances around them. If one cannot control what a mate *does,* then the next best thing is to attempt to change the temperament which *causes* the undesired actions, thereby ultimately achieving the desired goal.

Second, most people feel inwardly superior to those around them, secretly believing that their ways are best. Therefore, they want to change a mate so that he or she may be *comparable/alike* unto themselves. Also, they see it as a marvelous way of eliminating conflict.

Also, I believe the principle of "opposites attracting" is a deeply rooted phenomena placed within individuals as nature's way of balancing the scales in interpersonal relationships. I believe that humankind will never fully understand this "opposites attract" principle and all of its ramifications. Perhaps, it is simply further evidence of the Creator's way and will that is beyond our ability to explain, define, or categorize.

. . . about

FAMILY

"If we had paid no more attention to our plants than we have to our families, we would now be living in a jungle of weeds."

- Burbank

The Best Christmas Gift I Ever Received

I remember it as though it were yesterday. My daughter Sarah was in the second grade, and her teacher had told the children to make a paper doll of themselves as a gift for their parents. The end result was a labor of love, and I still have the paper statue, although Sarah is now 23 years old.

The "paper Sarah" is 13 inches tall, with blonde yarn tied into pigtails, held in place by brown yarn. The paper doll's eyes are not the same color as Sarah's, and they have these little lines coming from them like the long rays of sunlight that children depict in their drawings. I could never decide whether those lines were representing the sparkle she always had in her eyes, or whether they were representing her long eyelashes. The doll's face is pretty well shaped, although her nose is off-center, and her smile is crooked.

Her "dress" is made of green print wallpaper, with aqua lace trim and three mismatched buttons on the front. One button is green. One is blue. And the middle one has an aqua-marbled look with a white center. Although the buttons are in a very crooked line, they are pretty evenly spaced. And it was good that she put the *very* different button in the center.

The paper Sarah's face and arms are colored orange, her legs are green, and her feet are blue. The real Sarah was to write about herself inside on paper that had been cut the same shape as the wallpaper dress. She wrote the following in her very best printing:

> *Hello. My name is Sarah. I am 7 years old. I am a girl. My dog's name is Major. He barks a lot too. My Mom's name is Carol, and my brother's and Dad's name is Mark and David. I go to B.C.S. [Buechel Christian School]. I like my teacher. She is very very nice. Her name is Mrs. Riedling.*

It is not the most in-depth autobiographical sketch ever written. It contains a few grammatical errors. But it covers all the necessary important bases for a seven-year-old. She mentions herself, her age, her beloved pet, her family members, her school, and her much-loved teacher. We heard about Mrs. Riedling every evening. What she said. What she did. What she wore. How she talked. The stories she told. But most importantly, we heard about the love that Virginia Riedling showered upon each child. Her concern and appreciation for her students spilled over on a daily basis, and her students were drawn to her like a magnet. The children loved a teacher who *loved* them, as well as *taught* them. Virginia realized her twofold purpose in her students' lives.

As Christmas approached, Sarah came to me one afternoon and stretched out her little hands which held this wonderful "paper Sarah statue." She smiled her happiest smile, again revealing the fact that all four front teeth were missing. Her eyes danced with the excitement that only children can produce as they are about to offer a gift made with their own two little hands . . . an extension of themselves.

As she handed me this wonderful gift, she said, "Here, Mom, this is for you to look at when I'm in school." She knew, in her own seven-year-old way, that her mother thought about her and prayed for her during the day, even when separated by time and space. And this was her way of keeping us together when we were apart.

The paper doll's material value is probably only a few cents, if that.

But its true worth, measured in love, is beyond price.

Thank you, Sarah, for being my daughter.
I love you.
I trust that you will always want us to be together.
Perhaps not in body. Perhaps not in living space.
Perhaps not in the same town or even in the same state.
But always in spirit.

A Society without Porches

There are certain bastions of life that seem to represent much more than their individual existence. When we travel back in time to the days of our childhood, we remember the daily walks to our neighborhood school and the smell of home-baked cookies as we returned at the end of the day. We remember dinnertime as all members of the family gathered to share their day's activities. We remember being taught respect for other individuals and their property.

We remember doing business with the local merchants who knew us by name rather than by account numbers or credit cards. We remember picking up the telephone and hearing the operator greet us with "Number, please." We remember watching our mothers prepare meals before the days of TV dinners, instant mashed potatoes, and dehydrated vegetables.

We remember using our legs for transportation rather than expecting a car for our sixteenth birthday. We remember the numerous bus rides to town, for most families had only one automobile. And we remember the thrill of going to the movies rather than bringing the movies home to our own television set. But we do *not* remember microwave ovens, VCRs, and home computers.

And, significantly, we remember porches. Small porches. Big porches. Porches on the fronts of houses. Porches on the backs of houses. And *some* porches than ran along three sides of the house. Some of the porches had black iron railings. Some had wooden post railings. Some had brick posts. We could find various items on the porch, but we were certain of always finding two things in particular . . . a swing and a chair.

The swing and the chair were not simply ornamental pieces of porch furniture. They served a vital purpose. They were the vehicle through which members of the family would sit and discuss domestic matters of importance. The swing was the medium through which we would sit outdoors and watch the world go by . . . the squirrels playing tag in the yard, the rabbits playing hop scotch through the grass, and the children participating in their world of make-believe.

And it was through the swinging motion that we rocked our babies to sleep or rhythmically put the cares and frustrations of the day to rest. It was during the swing's back-and-forth movement that we privately communicated with ourselves and became familiar with our innermost thoughts.

The porches usually had little personal items on them as well. Perhaps a set of wind chimes through which we could enjoy nature's gentle song. Perhaps a small outdoor table where we could set a pretty pot of flowers or a glass of iced tea. Some porches even had small weather-resistant rugs that added the touch of family and friends as did the home itself.

And we could always find the mailbox on the porch. That gave us the perfect opportunity to converse with the mailman as he brought us the daily tidings from the world. He knew *our* name, and we knew *his*. We knew the mailman well enough that we could tell from his walk whether he was feeling especially chipper that day or whether his leather bag was especially burdensome.

It is true that our porches were an extension of the family life. It was as another room that needed cleaning, which added to our weekly chores . . . especially if our porch had one of those wooden slatted shades we could drop to keep out the hot afternoon sun or the evening rain or even, perhaps, the neighbor's chatter. But our porch was such a source of enjoyment, we did not mind. The porch was such a vital part of our home that we did not object to the extra responsibility of keeping it clean and inviting.

It was on these porches that personal problems were discussed and possible solutions were offered. It was where the news events of the world and the neighborhood were shared. It was where friends spent time becoming better acquainted. It was where children played under the close supervision of their parents, and where teenagers shared their deepest secrets and hopes with their friends. It was where neighbors, both young and old, sat to enjoy one another's wisdom and companionship.

Porches were, in essence, the focal point of American life . . . where conversations and relationships were born and developed.

But then America moved into the breakneck pace of the 1960's, and we no longer had time for porches. Husbands and wives couldn't afford the time for idle conversation, as each of them prepared for their next day's work in the factory or at the office. Parents no longer took the time to develop the bonds of expressed love or built the bridges of communication with their children. Siblings no longer had the opportunity to enjoy their brotherly or sisterly activities. All were consumed with doing as *much* as possible as *quickly* as possible.

As the annual family income rose, the desire for larger and more beautiful homes expanded. The new dwellings contained more square feet, larger windows, and more elegant features. The yard sizes shrunk as fewer working families created the opportunities for working in and around flower beds and vegetable gardens. Life became too hectic for personal fellowship outdoors. Neighborhood bonding lessened as families spent more hours working to pay for their finer homes and smaller yards.

And the porches?

They died a quiet and tragic death.

Thus, we have on today's American scene a nation of hurried and harried parents, lonely and hurting latchkey kids, and out-of-touch-with-each-other neighbors. We have children who do not know where their parents are. We have parents who do not know where their children are. We are raising a generation of young people who do not know *who* they are or *what* they are.

And many parents do not have the time to help them figure it out.

Millions of American homes and families have become dysfunctional in frighteningly disastrous ways. Young people are being handed over to teachers and preachers with the message from the parents, "Here, you fix them. We don't know what to do."

As adults, we have had time for so many activities and interests.

We have **not** had time for our children.

We have become a society without porches.

Children: America's Endangered Species

East Africa's Simien Fox is that country's endangered species. In the Asian mountains, the Snow Leopard tops the endangered list. The Mediterranean Monk Seal is at risk in the Mediterranean area. New Zealand's Forbes Parakeet is at risk. In South Brazil, it is the Woolly Spider Monkey. And in Indonesia, it is the Rothchild's Starling. In Mexico, the Volcano Rabbit is the endangered species.

"Endangered" is a term with which most of us are familiar, yet do we know its true meaning? According to the 1993 edition of Grollier World Encyclopedia of Endangered Species, it is defined as "A species in danger of extinction and whose survival seems improbable if factors that have put them at risk continue to affront them."

But we do not live in East Africa or New Zealand or Brazil or Indonesia or Mexico. We live in America.

What is *our* endangered species?

According to Grollier's definition, I believe we could quite accurately label our **children** as our nation's endangered species. Don't our children's safety and well-being face extinction if our society's factors that have put them at risk do not change? Under such circumstances, does their survival not seem improbable?

When thinking of an animal's survival, we tend to consider such elements as food supply, water, living accommodations, climatic conditions, disease, and poachers.

Children's survival is no less dependent upon certain elements within their world, also. What are those aspects of today's society that threaten the very lives of our children?

2 8

TOBACCO. The U.S. Department of Education recently released figures that reveal 25% of Americans, many of whom are teens, smoke cigarettes on a regular basis and that the annual estimated number of cigarette-induced deaths is 50,000. Since recent evidence seems to indicate the addictive nature of nicotine, it is understandable that fewer than 20 percent of 1,000 tested smokers succeeded in their goal to quit smoking on the first attempt. In addition, smokers are more likely than nonsmokers to suffer from such ailments as heart disease, along with cancer of the lungs, bladder, larynx, and esophagus.

ALCOHOL. Again, with statistics from the U.S. Department of Education, we know that alcohol is the leading drug problem among youths. In a University of Michigan report titled "Monitoring the Future," new information was released concerning the widespread use of alcohol among teens. Consider the following percentage figures of alcohol consumption for the following grades:

	8th graders	10th graders	12th graders
1992-94	49%	67%	75%

(last years for which figures are available)

This increasing alcohol epidemic has been accomplished through such measures as widespread acceptability, extensive promotion, and easy accessibility. A large consumption of alcohol is frequently accompanied by poor nutrition, and the combination of these two situations can lead to permanent damage of vital organs. Even low doses of alcohol can result in impaired judgment and coordination, varying degrees of aggressive acts (which can result in child and/or spouse abuse), and diminished learning and memory capabilities.

TEEN PREGNANCY. In the 1995 edition of the Statistical Abstract of the United States, reports reveal that for every 8,000 Caucasian pregnancies (under 15 years of age), there are 14,000 Black pregnancies, and 5,000 Hispanic pregnancies. In the 15-19 year age group, the statistics reveal quite a different profile. In that age group, for every 489,000 Caucasian pregnancies, there are 272,000 Black pregnancies, and 177,000 Hispanic pregnancies. Many pregnant teens are opting to keep their babies, often at the expense of their education. This lack of education, which leads to fewer employment opportunities, results in a staggering and swelling welfare program. Added to this financial disaster is the frightening prospect of these babies being raised by young parents who frequently have poor parenting skills. And considering that these children will learn their own parenting skills from their ill-prepared parents, the cycle continues.

ILLICIT DRUG USE. In a recent study from the University of Michigan Institute for Social Research, we learn the following percentages of graduating class members who used cocaine and crack, two of the most deadly drugs:

	Cocaine	Crack
class of '75	9%	
'80	15.7%	
'86	16.9%	
'87		5.4%
'88		4.8%
'90	9.4%	3.5%
'91		3.1%
'92	6.1%	2.6%
'93	6.1%	2.6%
'94	5.9%	3.0%

As we look at this percentage table, we may find ourselves feeling a false sense of security in the declining percentage rates. But we must remember that the population is increasing, thereby increasing the actual number of teen drug cases.

SEXUALLY TRANSMITTED DISEASES. The 15-19-year age group is the second highest group in the U.S., with more than 60 percent of all *new* STD cases being in the 15-24-year age group.

CHILD ABUSE/NEGLECT. According to the National Center on Child Abuse Prevention Research, child abuse was formally recognized by the medical profession as the "battered child syndrome" in 1961. But since 1985, the number of such cases has risen 50 percent. According to this research program, there are four basic reasons for this increase, including the following: increased public awareness of the situation (resulting in an increased number of reported cases); more families living at or near poverty level (thereby increasing stress levels); abuse of alcohol and other substances (resulting in irresponsible behavior); and fewer resources available for the increased number of families who need child protective services (resulting from the three situations listed above).

In 1993, the National Committee to Prevent Child Abuse reported that an approximate 2.9 million children were identified as victims of either child abuse or child neglect. This figure translates into 45 children out of every 1,000 being mistreated either actively or passively. We are abusing the very core of our future in ways that may never be remedied. And as abused children, they are much more likely to be abusive parents themselves.

DEPRESSION. According to an April, 1995, report by the National Institute of Child Health and Human Development, 5 percent of America's teens suffer from clinical depression. Although that percentage may seem small at first glance, it represents 250,000 American teenagers dealing with this problem. The same report continues on to tell us that of every 200 teenage girls ages 12-18, one of them will suffer from depression to some degree. And lest we think of depression as a feminine gender sickness, we must remember that 6 percent of teenage patients are male.

EATING DISORDERS. The U.S. Department of Health tells us that 2-3 percent of American adolescent girls suffer from bulimia, with a fewer number of males suffering from the disorder. Such individuals experience frequent and uncontrollable periods of eating, followed by purging of their bodies, either by induced vomiting or ingesting large amounts of laxatives. An additional 1 percent of patients' cases develop into full anorexia nervosa, which results in refusal to eat. Psychologists state that both bulimia and anorexia have their roots in emotional difficulties.

YOUTH SUICIDES. In an April, 1995, report from the U.S. Center for Disease Control and Prevention, we learn that suicides by children 10 to 14 years of age have increased at twice the rates as in 1980. According to this report, guns were the most frequently used method of suicide, for a total of 65 percent. The report also points out that, although the number of young people attempting suicide has not increased, "successful" suicides have risen due to the more lethal means being employed. From 1980 to 1992, increased suicide rates for adolescents between the ages of 10 and 14 have increased 86 percent for white boys, 233 percent for white girls, 300 percent for black boys, and 100 percent for black girls. There were no numbers for Hispanics available in this portion of the report.

DIVORCE/ONE-PARENT FAMILIES. As the rate of U.S. divorce has reached epidemic proportions, those couples who remain married to their original spouse now rank in the minority. Two out of every three marriages now end in divorce court, with the children involved being the greatest victims. Due to the high emotional level involved in the breakup of a marriage, children are often exposed to the parents' arguments, concerning material possessions *and* the children themselves. Visitation and custody arrangements are often the result of each parent wanting to hurt the other, with the children being caught directly in the line of fire.

Communication between ex-spouses is often inadequate or hurtful, with the children feeling they must be the detail-organizers or peacemakers. Children are often left feeling they must defend the one parent during a verbal attack from the other parent. In an attempt to win the children's "love," one or both parents will permit the children to have broad or few limitations placed upon them. However, to the children, this translates into a lack of concern *and* love . . . the very things the parents are trying to win. Children are heard saying across the nation, "My parents don't care about me. They let me do anything I want."

And in the midst of these emotional battles, the children are left feeling as though they are "prizes" or "trophies" to be won by the highest bidder. According to the January, 1995, census information, there are 46 metropolitan areas with one million or more people. Of these areas, New York led the way with 36 percentage of homes being single-parent. New Orleans was second with 34 percent, Miami with 31 percent, Detroit with 29 percent, and Sacramento and Baltimore (each with 28 percent) followed respectively. The census report also showed that 40 percent of single-parent home/apartment *renters* were either unemployed or not in the labor force, as opposed to 16 percent of single-parent home *owners.*

Yes, we are concerned for all endangered species . . . the foxes, the leopards, the seals, the parakeets, the spiders, the starlings, and the rabbits. We are concerned that such animals have sufficient food supplies, clean drinking water, adequate living accommodations, proper climatic conditions, less disease, and fewer poachers.

But our hearts should be breaking. And our souls should be searching . . . attempting to find ways, whatever the cost, of saving our most precious of all endangered species . . . our children! They are our greatest natural resource . . . our future! They also need adequate food, water, clothing, and shelter.

But they *cannot* and *will not* survive without love and nurturing and support and instruction and encouragement.

And where will they learn all this?

From us . . . Their examples.

We must realize . . .

If we fail in our responsibility,

OUR WORLD FAILS!

I Shall Never Forget My Way Home

My childhood days were filled with the usual *kid* things . . . scrapes with the sidewalk, splinters from the telephone poles I slid down at breakneck speed, bruises from jumping fences, and colds from running in the rain and snow with no shoes.

I treasured picking wild violets along the side of the road with my mother. I recall the process of hanging clothes on the line to dry, sprinkling them with water from a glass coke bottle, rolling them up and putting them in a plastic bag for later treatment, and putting them in the refrigerator if the ironing was to be completed several hours later.

I remember my dad bringing the Beagles home from hunting and how he lovingly checked their feet for thorns and rubbed their ears and tails with olive oil to promote healing of the scratches caused by briars. I also remember how he lifted the dogs from the truck to the pen when they were too tired to jump.

I remember walking down the street to my grandparents' home and hiding under the dining room table to surprise Grandpap when he came home from working at the steel mill. And I can still smell the flowers as Grandma and I would sit in the back porch swing and talk about so many things. I remember something else about Grandma, too . . . she would never allow me to do anything she knew my mother wouldn't permit. I heard other kids talking about *their* grandparents allowing them to do ANYTHING they wanted, and I couldn't understand why MY grandmother couldn't be that way. But now I understand. She knew that if she permitted a double standard, I would work her against my mother. And Grandma was far too smart for that!

I remember the days of wooden ironing boards, wringer-type washing machines, metal rinse tubs, and liquid bluing in the rinse water to make clothes whiter. I never did figure that one out . . . adding blue to make something white! And I can still smell the dust from the coal being dropped into the coal cellar in our basement. I never liked going in there. It was sooo dirty! It was also cold! But it made a wonderful storage place for the apples to be kept in the fall and winter months.

I remember that coal cellar door, too. It was made from roughly cut wooden slats that were held together with cross boards nailed in place. And the door "latch" was simply a block of wood loosely nailed to the door frame. All one had to do to make it work was turn the wooden block; even a kid like me could do it.

A funny thing about that coal cellar, though. It was located in the basement near the furnace. On the one side of that slatted door was the warmth and coziness of the furnace heat. But on the other side was that penetrating cold from the coal storage area. Two different worlds . . . such a study in contrasts. And the only thing that separated them was that old wooden door!

Of course, my *dreams* took me to far away lands where I was a princess living in a spectacular mansion, dressed in finest silk, riding in my satin-lined carriage and being waited upon by my servants. No such things as dirty clothes, school, or chores in my dream world.

But, of course, one cannot remain a child forever; I entered my teens. My curiosity led me into several narrow escapes with tragedy, and my rebellion acquainted me with learning many lessons the hard way because I knew I could learn nothing from my parents. Anything they had to say certainly would be outdated and narrow-minded. I knew the greatest trial of being a teen was coping with Mother and Daddy.

Aspirations for the future began to invade my thought life, and I started to think of the life's work for which I would be most suited.

I enjoyed being with people and giving advice, so perhaps counseling was my calling. I also enjoyed working with hair, so

I gave thought to becoming a stylist. The idea of public relations appealed to me, for I enjoyed nice dinners in fancy restaurants. What I did *not* have was the stomach for blood and pain. That ruled out the nursing profession. But that decision created a real dilemma for me; most of my friends were choosing nursing school. It was the early 1960's, and society still expected me to enter either the secretarial pool, nursing school, or the educational field. How could I even *think* of being a teacher? I had spent 12 years in a classroom, and I could not imagine myself being on the other side of the teacher's desk. Besides, I always hated chalk dust!

After a whirlwind of applications, decisions, and packing, I found myself away at college. Suddenly I didn't have any clean clothes unless I washed them. I no longer had the delightful experience of walking into the kitchen and smelling home-cooked food. The campus cafeteria somehow left something to be desired. And I never could tolerate eating my meals from those ugly brown trays. My idea of fun and games went out the window as tests and term papers started. The preparation had begun, and the evaluation of *ME* soon followed.

Four years later, I was married and teaching in a classroom. The students were great, the textbooks were average, and my colleagues seemed so much older and wiser than myself. I wondered if I had bitten off more than I could chew! As I learned to live with my husband on a personal basis and work with my fellow male teachers on a professional basis, I continued to wonder how men and women could be created so differently and yet be expected to live together in peace and harmony.

Travel included a summer mission trip to a small Central American country where poverty was the rule, and proper sanitation the dream of everyone. The only clock was the sun, and the only goal was to survive.

Then in my married life, the children arrived. Starting a family had seemed easy before, but then it was always happening to *someone else*. Now it was my turn, and the task of raising a child into an independently functioning human being seemed overwhelming. The job was often frustrating, yet it was so filled with joy and rewards. The pleasure of seeing children perform their daily routine with such openness and honesty was like a breath of fresh air. It was definitely worth the hassle!

My life's journey has taken me to many places, introduced me to many people, and exposed me to many situations. The excursion has lasted over half a century and has often led me far from that small place on the map where I first began.

It may not be the most technologically advanced city in the state.

It may not be the cleanest town in the country.

It may not have the greatest employment opportunities.

But it is where I started.

And I shall never forget my way home!

. . . about
NATURE

"Nature and wisdom always
say the same."
- Juvenal

March Marches In

Ask any calendar-minded person to name the third month of the year, and the response will be "March." However, under the ancient Roman calendar, March (honoring Mars, the Roman god of war) was the *first* month; the revision came later under the edict of emperor Julius Caesar who decreed that each new year would begin with January.

Although no national holidays occur in March, it is a month filled with many notable occasions, including the following: Texas won independence from Mexico in 1836, inventor Alexander Graham Bell was born in 1847, American football coach Knute Rockne was born in 1888, Eli Whitney invented the cotton gin in 1794, Julius Caesar was assassinated in 44 B.C., Patrick Henry declared, "Give me liberty, or give me death" in 1775, and German physicist Wilhelm Roentgen (who discovered X rays) was born in 1845.

Not only have numerous historical events occurred during this month, but several old sayings are also associated with it. Perhaps the most common adage concerning March is that it "comes in like a lion, and goes out like a lamb," referring to the fact that weather at the first of March is usually blustery, windy, and cold. But by the end of the month, weather patterns have generally become milder, calmer, and warmer.

Many farmers believe the old superstition that if rain falls on the first three days of March, crops will be poor. Some farmers believe this so strongly, they will not plant during this time if such weather conditions exist.

Although the violet is the official flower for March, other bits of budding creatures begin to make their presence known. As one begins to watch closely for the first specks of color after a possibly drab winter, hearts are warmed to once again realize that beneath the cold, frozen soil has been lying *life*.

Life that, although dormant and quiet in recent months, is ready to spring forth with color and beauty.

Life that is ready to shout to the world, "Hey, I'm here! Let's get growing!"

Have you ever noticed that the first flower on your property somehow seems special, although others soon follow? Is it possibly our way of welcoming in the first breath of life at the start of another growing season?

As the hibernating animals emerge from their winter dens, let us humans take time to enjoy the emerging beauty the earth is producing. Take time to leisurely walk through the woods and appreciate the shades of green as they replace the boring browns and tans.

Escape the hectic pace of daily life and retreat to a place of solitude where we hear no sounds but those of nature. Let us temporarily isolate ourselves from constant professional and personal demands as we allow our inner self to become rejuvenated and appreciative of the things around us that we so often take for granted.

Take the time to sit by a quiet stream and watch a fallen leaf make its way privately down its watery trail. Or view the stream from differing vantage points and become aware of the varying colors of the water as it makes its way over the rocks from different angles. Sit so quietly that the woodland creatures will venture close, unaware of a foreign presence in their world.

Let each of us step back into our childhood and walk in the rain, remembering the thrill of raindrops hitting our face. Remember how much fun it was catching the drops on your tongue? Do it again, and forget about the hair stringing into your face, or the clothes soaking onto your body. Watch the squirrels scampering around the trees, envy the rabbits contentedly munching on sweet grass, and laugh at the smug little "grins" painted on the faces of the chipmunks.

Experience the joy and anticipation of new life as you concentrate on the mother bird, her body full of eggs whose shells nurture the young ones within her. Focus on her methodical and determined efforts in preparing her family's *home*. And if Mother Nature would be so gracious, allow yourself the pleasure and education of watching those eggs hatch as baby birds emerge . . . babies whose only thoughts seem to focus on eating. Notice the changes as the scrawny, bony bodies become protected with feathers that seem lighter than air.

But if you look too closely, prepare yourself for an attack from Mother Bird; she does not know you are merely observing. If you invade the territory that houses her precious young, she will spring into action as would any mother. She will attack with a viciousness that is oblivious to the size or weight difference between herself and you. Her sole concern is to protect her offspring, and she will do so at any cost.

We observe small children playing, and we wish we could go back again to the carefree days of childhood innocence. We cannot turn back our biological clocks, but we *can* reverse our train of thought if we so desire. We have responsibilities to our world, and we cannot shirk those responsibilities. But we do have the right and the freedom to allow ourselves to be our own person and to enjoy our own *selfhood*. We must remember that if we do not take care of ourselves, we cannot take care of those around us.

And so as "March Marches In," may we have the curiosity and courage to alter our customary path of daily activity. Be willing to march to the beat of a different seasonal drummer, and thoroughly enjoy the bounty of today.

A gift that is beyond price!

Spring is Sprung!

Those funny little lines we pull from our memory. We can't remember where we first heard them, but we still enjoy the rhyming humor of "Spring is sprung; the grass is ris'. I wonder where the daisies is!"

We look around our world in the springtime and try to saturate our senses with all the stimulation we can find as we use the five senses most of us possess (hearing, seeing, touching, smelling, and tasting). We tend to take them for granted until we are asked to focus upon them for a moment.

As we pause for a moment to be grateful for these five blessings, we think of our heightened sense of hearing. Steal a few minutes of time for yourself, and slip away to a quiet place . . . a place that does not know the sounds of screeching automobiles, barking dogs, and shouting children. Find the quietest place possible, and begin to listen.

Listen to WHAT?

Perhaps the rustle of a leaf, or the whistle of a breeze, or perhaps the sound of your own heartbeat. If we listen closely enough, we may hear the very sound of silence . . . . Listen! . . . . Can you hear it? Can you describe it? Doesn't it seem to have an existence all of its very own? And what price tag could we place on the privilege of hearing our child's first cry or hearing that special someone say "I love you."

What did you think about the last time you heard a beloved pet's rhythmic breathing as he curled up beside you? What went through your mind as you last listened to a loved one's snoring, realizing what deathly quiet its absence would bring? Have you realized what you would have missed if you had not heard your friend's sincere apologetic words of "I'm sorry"? Do you remember the comfort those words brought when you realized the true repentance they represented, and that it was the beginning of the healing process in your relationship?

See WHAT?

Our sense of sight is delighted as we soak in the beauty of a multitude of flowers, each with individual colors and shapes. We watch as the brown grasses of winter take on the green hues that add such variety to the surrounding landscape. Our eyes sparkle with delight as we witness young animals learning to fend for themselves as they watch their parents. Oh, the joy of seeing a young colt run through the pasture as though the world were his, yet always making certain his mother is not far away.

And who could put into words the amusement of watching small children discover each little object in their world. Is it possible to imagine a world consisting only of black as one goes from day to day. No red. No green. No yellow. No pastels. No neon colors. Only black!

Feel WHAT?

Our sense of touch is generally given little consideration until we injure a part of our body, and then it seems as though every nerve in our body focuses upon that injury. Try to imagine, if you can, being denied the experience of feeling a satin cloth or a velvet rose. Imagine life without the ability to distinguish the feel of a puppy's soft ears from the feel of a burlap potato sack. Even thorns and grains of sand hold their own identity and words of caution. Remove the sand from your shoe and avoid the thorns, or there *will* be a price to pay.

Can you recall the first time you walked along the beach and felt the wet sand squish between your toes? Can you recreate the occasion when you initially dipped your toes into that cold mountain stream? The cutting iciness was so intense, you thought surely you could pick up the coldness and hold it in your hand. But we can only *feel* cold, not touch it. Select a rough dry pebble lying in the dirt, along with a smooth stone lying under water. Run your fingers over them and attempt to find descriptive words that properly portray their distinctive characteristics. Think you can easily do it without the sense of touch? Put on a glove and attempt to pick up a pin or a single blade of grass.

Feel the wonderfully soft skin of a baby and appreciate the newness and innocence it represents. Or feel the wrinkled skin of an older loved one and ponder the experience and wisdom of which it speaks. Consider the age lines and think of the many acts of kindness they represent.

Smell WHAT?

Our sense of smell is closely related to our ability to taste, and what affects the one often affects the other. Those individuals who have suffered certain types of head trauma report smelling smells that do not exist in their world at that time. Cinnamon may smell like chicken soup, or the satisfying aromas of cologne and bubble bath may not exist at all to such individuals.

Imagine being denied the thrill of smelling roasting turkey at Thanksgiving or the drifting waves of baked ham at Easter. How would one feel being denied the treat of smelling a home-baked pie in the oven . . . or a cooling carrot cake on the kitchen counter top?

And what of the time when your sense of smell saved your home? When your nose told you that electrical wiring was beginning to burn, or that your gas water heater was leaking.

And we can never forget when our sense of smell saved our babies from living another minute with a dirty diaper!

Taste WHAT?

Yes, the sense of taste. How we equate taste with comfort and enjoyment. How limited life would seem without indulging in the tartness of green apples, the spice of pumpkin pie, or the saltiness of peanuts and potato chips. Imagine eating a new vegetable and not knowing whether it was similar to green beans or home grown corn. And the onion . . . is it strong and hot, or is it sweet and enjoyable? And what about that delectable treat of pepperoni pizza?

If we were forced to choose which sense we must forfeit, which one would we select? Would the four remaining ones be somehow diminished without the existence of the fifth one? Or would the remaining four be strengthened in an attempt to compensate for the lost sense?

Five blessings.

We use them each day.

But we do not focus upon them

until we are asked to do so.

Those Beautiful Shells

My friend Christie Dalton was recently preparing to vacation in Florida, and I casually asked her to bring back some sea shells for me. We have many lakes and rivers here in Kentucky, but we do *not* have many sea shells. We have plenty of fresh water here in the Blue Grass state, but we don't have much salt water!

As a professional woman, Christie is always busy juggling home, family, and professional responsibilities. I felt certain she would forget my request in the midst of her hectic schedule. But upon her return, she cheerfully told me she had a bag full of shells and that they had been picked by her *personally* from the gulf water. I was so excited and could hardly wait to see them! Isn't it funny what little things bring out the childlike happiness in otherwise adult humans? I have always seemed to have an abundance of happy feelings. I hope I never lose them.

As I went to claim my treasure, I was delighted to find shells . . . *lots* of shells . . . lots of different *kinds* of shells . . . lots of different *colors* of shells. And each one seemed to have an individual character.

As I look at these sea shells tonight, I wish they could talk. I would ask them how long they had been around, where they had been, what they had experienced, who they had met. You know, the usual questions you ask sea shells. I would ask them about their world where the land and the sea meet. Have you ever thought about what it would be like to live somewhere that, at high tide, your land home becomes the ocean . . . and at low tide, the same area again becomes part of the land? Talk about a changing environment!

I would ask the shells which of the three types of seashores they came from . . .

a rocky shore,

a muddy shore,

or a sandy shore.

One shell, the "horn of plenty" shape we often see, looks like he's had a rough life. His wraparound edge is jagged and sharp, and he suffers from various holes and cracks. There's not much color, but there's a lot of character. His rough, bleached-white external surface is filled with lines and swirls, but his internal surface is smooth and shiny. Why is that? Why are the insides of such shells so glossy and smooth? It seems like a study in contradiction.

Near the top of the worn-out shell, where the tightening swirl becomes much smaller, there is a dark little mass. The space is too small for me to see it clearly, and I certainly don't want to stick something inside the shell to break it loose. I might break the shell. And then the magic would be gone. So I plan to just leave the shell as it is and wonder about it for a while.

Two other shells, shaped differently from the horn of plenty one, look as though they could be related. They are the same size, the same shape, the same basic color, and have the same shaped hole near the small end of them. One is a little more gray the other one, but perhaps that's because he's older. The other one is definitely a blonde!

There is a smaller third shell shaped exactly like the second two, but he is in much better shape. He has more color than the other two, and his colors are more brilliant. He also does not have any holes in him. He must have lived the easy life! He's prettier than the other two, but he just doesn't seem to have as much character. Perhaps there is a parallel here. Perhaps a harder life *does* make us more interesting.

And then there is a fourth shell that's between the size of the first two and the third one. He doesn't have any gaping holes, but he is filled with holes ranging from pencil-lead to pin-point size.

It looks like he's been around and suffered some scars in the process.

There are two smaller horn-of-plenty shaped shells that are approximately the same size. But the similarity ends there. The light peach porcelain-looking one has more of itself *missing* than present. The outside is beautifully striped. But the inside is pure, glossy white.

The accompanying gray friend is slightly larger and rugged looking from the get-go. He's thick, all intact, and has that rugged he-man look. And when I turned him upside down just now, lots of sand fell onto my computer desk where I am working. Just think, Florida sand and Kentucky computer technology are joined together. I think I'll save the sand as an extra memento from Christie.

My daughter brought me some sand and shells from her trip to Florida a few years ago, and I have them in a beveled glass container in the family room. But *those* shells and sand look different from *these*. I guess sand and shells are like people.

All of them are different.

Then there is a wonderful assortment of smaller shells, all basically the same shape but of different colors, textures, and character lines. Some are solid colored. Some are speckled. Some are striped. Some have deep contour lines. Some have shallow lines. All very much the same, yet so completely different.

Perhaps if I talk to the shells (like we are supposed to talk to plants), they will give up some of their secrets.

Perhaps they will tell me how long they have been around, where they have been, what they have experienced, and whom they have met. You know, the usual answers that sea shells give people.

Look! Up in the Sky!

"Star light. Star bright. First star I've seen tonight. I wish I may. I wish I might. Have the wish I wish tonight."

A little rhyme from childhood that has lingered through adulthood.

It was most likely one of the first little poems we learned as children. As we began our first faltering steps as infants, we glued our eyes to the ground as we attempted to coordinate vision and walking. We scanned the earth for stones to snatch, roots to step over, sidewalk cracks to avoid, and ants to catch.

But somewhere along the way we became aware of a broader dimension to our world, and we began looking around. We first saw things nearby, but one night something magical happened. Our eyes wandered heavenward, and we were astonished at the sight we beheld. As we peered into the darkness above us, we were overwhelmed by the beauty that quietly awaited someone's notice in the darkness on high. From that blackness came twinkles, sparkles, flickers, and blinks that magically popped from the drab celestial ceiling overhead.

It was probably on this day (or rather *night*) of our life that we first heard "Twinkle, Twinkle, Little Star." We had no idea what "twinkle" meant. All we knew was that we were watching something wonderful and different from anything we had ever seen in the daylight. And the quietness made the wonder seem even more magical. Perhaps we thought that if we reached high enough, we could touch one of those glittering little specks.

After all, they couldn't be very large.

They were just a tiny spot in that big, big sky!

Then we started attending school and, somewhere along the line, we began learning all the required "scientific stuff" about stars. We discovered that stars are actually huge balls of fire . . .

5 1

glowing gas in the sky. We were amazed to learn that the sun is also a star. We had a hard time understanding that because the sun certainly doesn't *look* like a star. That's because the sun is the only star close enough to the earth to *look* like a ball. And the sun is 93 *million* miles away!

We also learned that:

— there are about 200 billion stars in the universe.

— a star's composition is approximately 75% hydrogen, 22% helium, and 3% other chemicals.

— stars' sizes range from 1/50th to 50 times the mass of the sun.

— stars' colors range from blue through white, yellow, and orange to red, depending on the star's surface temperature.

— the farthest stars are in galaxies *billions* of light years away.

That last fact is especially mind-boggling when one stops to consider that light travels at 186,000 miles *per second!* So multiply 186,000 times 60 (seconds per minute) times 60 (minutes per hour) times 24 (hours per day) times 365 (days per year), and you will have the distance of a star that is *one light-year* away! And we are talking *thousands* and *millions* of light-years in distance!

Our math capabilities allow us to see the actual numbers involved in our calculations, but can we truly understand the magnitude of such distance and space? Some stars are so far away that, by the time their light travels close enough to the earth for us to see, the star itself has been destroyed. So we are actually seeing the light from something that no longer exists! And we, as intelligent humans, think we have a "handle" on things!

So much for the scientific aspect of the heavens. Let us think again about the special beauty and magic of those things we call stars. Treat yourself to a special time. Get away from the glow of city lights, take a blanket or chair, and rest yourself somewhere out in nature. Lie back, allow your mind to wander, enjoy yourself, and just experience being "under the stars." Look at the blackness (which will become more detailed the longer you look), listen to the quietness (which can become very intense), and come to appreciate the orderliness and greatness of the created world in which we live.

There is a part of a song that occasionally dances its way through my mind. I don't remember the title or the artist, but it tells us to "Catch a falling star, and put it in your pocket. Save it for a rainy day. Catch a falling star, and put it in your pocket. Never let it fade away. No matter what . . . ." I don't recall the rest of it, but it was a catchy little tune that had a way of lifting one's spirits on a dreary day. Again, the magic of stars!

A young lady whom I have known since the day she was born, was recently asked to write a personal piece of writing for a university class. This young woman is a very special part of my life. She shares my last name, lives in my home, and occupies a large portion of my heart. Within moments, she penned the following:

STARS

I've heard what they say:

Stars are nothing more
than immense balls of gas
and dust.
They shimmer for a while
and then they are gone as the gas
slowly burns to extinction.

Stars are what we see
>   after the sun goes to sleep
>   and the moon comes out to play.

But when I look up, I see ---
>   **Chandeliers** hanging
>   in a majestic ballroom,
>   lighting the way for the planets
>   as they dance in their orbits.
>   **Campfires** of the ones
>   gone on before.
>   **Guides** which lead you safely home
>   when you seem to lose your way.
>   **Lullaby characters**
>   peering mysteriously
>   down from the sky.

Stars link two hearts
>   torn apart by the miles.

Stars are God's way
>   of reminding me
>   that He is always near.

But the most beautiful of all:
>   Stars are the sparkle
>   in a baby's eyes
>   who will one day exclaim,
>   **"Daddy . . . fireflies!"**

- Sarah E. Heizer

And There They Stood!

We were horseback riding that evening, not really expecting anything special. We had been over the trail many times and had even laughed about being able to follow it in our sleep. Of course the scenery would differ from season to season, and we would occasionally stumble upon someone enjoying a nature walk. But nothing much out of the ordinary happened during these mother-daughter rides. We were enjoying each other's company as we took pleasure in the horses' companionship also.

We had started our ride at the barn (but then I guess that's where *most* horse rides begin, come to think of it). The horses were showing their usual eagerness to break away and canter for a while. They seemed to enjoy the straight stretches where they could exercise their lungs. But they also seemed to enjoy the more rugged parts of the terrain where they could snatch a few bites of honeysuckle along the way.

I often wondered what those horses thought as we rode them through the woods. Could they read our thoughts and somehow know in advance which path we would take? Could they sense our joy at being out in the woods, in touch with nature, away from the sights and sounds of humanity for a brief time? Did they ever wonder what was troubling us as we occasionally used these rides for relaxing in an attempt to deal with daily stresses of living in the twentieth century? Did they ever understand our love for them as our relationship grew over the years? Did they ever sense our concern over feeling that occasionally something just wasn't quite right in the woods? I wonder if *they* knew what that *something* was?

Buck loved pieces of pepper mint and sugar cubes. He also enjoyed MacDonald's hamburgers, but he would always manage to spit the pickle out without losing the rest of the sandwich. We never did figure how he managed that. He was also health conscious because he enjoyed apples and carrots. I was grateful to have an animal that was so concerned for his physical well-being. Since he ate well, received sufficient exercise, drank plenty of water, didn't smoke or drink alcoholic beverages, and received all the loving care an animal could ever desire, I felt sure he would live forever.

Our ride had been especially fun that evening, for we had gone to the creek where Buck loved to play. I'm sure it sounds strange to say that a horse liked to *play,* but it was true. He would lower his head as far as possible into the creek, swish it around, then let it come flying up . . . spraying water on himself and anyone else within close proximity. A few times I thought I almost detected a smile on his face. I don't know . . . can horses smile?

The creek water ran only 12-18 inches deep, and there was no concern for anyone "getting in over their head." But there was sufficient water for the horses to paw and splash. And paw and splash they did. We stayed on the horses during all of this, and we always came away with horse, rider, and tack covered with water. But it was worth the fun.

When Buck would emerge from his *wading pool* experience, he would be energized as though charged with electricity. The cold creek water seemed to liven his spirits as nothing else could do. As a rider, one could feel the energy racing through his body and simply went along for the ride as the four-legged creature enjoyed his world to the fullest. Our evening had been wonderful, and we couldn't have asked for anything better. But Mother Nature had a surprise in store.

We were on the last quarter mile of the ride, heading for the barn. A rider must always be careful at this point, for it is a horse's nature to break away and run that last distance home where he can relax and snooze. But instead of the horses wanting to charge full steam ahead, they stopped in mid-stride. It was such an unusual behavior that both my daughter and I sat motionless, trying to see what would make the animals behave in such a manner.

It was dusk, the sky was beautiful with shades of red and orange and yellow, and the smell of the evening mist was becoming evident. In a matter of seconds, it seemed that the entire world had stopped. My daughter and I hesitated to even breathe, let alone move. Buck's nostrils flared, his ears were standing ever so straight in the air, his head was slightly cocked, and I could feel his breathing and heartbeat becoming more rapid.

We knew we were part of something very special, and we continued to watch, being careful not to move and frighten whatever it was that we were about to witness.

Finally we saw!

And there they stood!

A doe and her two little fawns. My, those fawns were little. The littlest I'd ever seen. We realized for the first time that *she* was watching *us* as intently as *we* were now watching *her* and her babies! I knew from having been the daughter and the wife of a hunter that I could not look those lovely animals directly in the eye. That spooks wild animals, and they always run. And I didn't want anything to shorten this wonderful moment in time.

Had those deer stumbled into our world, or had we stumbled into theirs? It really didn't matter, for the magic of the moment erased all reason. The wonder of seeing nature at its finest took precedence over everything else. I don't know how much time passed. It seemed like only seconds, yet hours, all at the same time.

No one moved for the longest time. Not my daughter. Not her horse. Not myself. Not Buck. And not the doe. The little fawns didn't seem quite so concerned, but that's typical of children.

They don't worry much because mom and dad are supposed to have everything under control.

As I sat transfixed, I marveled at those little fawns whom nature had so beautifully camouflaged with their coloring and spots. One had to practically run over them before realizing they were even present. I wanted to simultaneously run and pick one of them up, yet not interfere in any way with the wonder before me.

And then I watched the doe. Her huge brown eyes reminded me of glistening brown diamonds . . . not appearing to move, yet taking in every detail in the world around her.

Quick as a flash, Mama Deer turned tail and vanished into the woods, with the little ones scampering in hot pursuit. They weren't about to be left behind! Where *Mama* went, *they* went. The three of them disappeared without a sound, and I found myself wondering . . . how can something move that quickly, yet not make a single noise?

And in a moment as quick as the twinkling of an eye, the magic moment of human and animal unexpectedly meeting was ended. They would go on their way in a world that was familiar to them. And we would go on our way in a world that was familiar to us.

Nothing had changed.

Yet nothing seemed quite the same.

. . . about

EDUCATION

"Education is the mirror of
society."

- Eld

The Teacher Learned . . . Again!

The following scenario is often presented to new teachers entering a classroom situation:

You can't ever let them get the upper hand on you, or you're finished. So start out tough. The first day you enter a new class, let them know who's boss. You've got to start out tough, then you ease up as you go along. If you start out easygoing, when you try to get tough, they'll just look at you and laugh.

This was the advice given to my husband and me during new teacher orientation back in 1967. Only the principal emphasized the original message by adding, "Don't smile until Christmas." We both looked upon this man as a professional person with many years of experience who *must* know how to handle children. Thus, we followed his advice.

At the time, I was teaching middle school, and the above approach appeared to work well. I had no discipline problems and no class disruptions. But I also had no student creativity **or** teacher enjoyment. However, I wasn't sensitive to the lack of creativity and enjoyment. I was so pleased with my beautifully controlled classroom that I thought I was the perfect teacher.

After quite some time of this dictatorship approach, I came to realize that, yes, I had a well-controlled classroom. But it was borne out of fear. I also realized that where that amount of fear resides, there can be no real respect or harmony. And there can be no genuine interpersonal relationship between teacher and student. At about the same time I began having these meaningful revelations, I resigned from teaching to start my family.

Ten years went by, and I was ready to re-enter the teaching profession. At this point, I was beginning to teach high school, and I was greeted with the following warning from my principal:

"Be careful. This is a tough group, and they are ready to go after a new teacher. They have run off the last two English teachers." Without even giving conscious thought to it, I kicked myself into dictator overdrive again. As I look back, I cannot believe I made the same stupid mistake *twice* in my professional life!

I had a very difficult year with that particular group, and only through a courageous student who came to me at the end of the year, did I realize the magnitude of my mistake. He confronted me with the following statement: "Mrs. Heizer, when you came here, we decided to run you off like the last two teachers before you. We were ready, but you came in that first day as though you were ready to kill bears. We decided then and there that you were not going to run like the others. So we didn't try. We just decided to make your life miserable."

He was right. I didn't run. He was right again. They made my life miserable that year. Through my conversations with Tim, I told him how much I appreciated his honesty and courage. I also told him I realized I had gone beyond *firm* into *mean* in my attempt to control. In doing so, by both verbal and nonverbal communication, I had thrown out challenge after challenge to my students to undermine and attack my authority. I hadn't viewed those students as a source of enjoyment. I had seen them as the adversary.

I learned a great deal from that experience. I learned to be firm, yet kind; expecting, yet not demanding; courteous and friendly, yet expecting respect. In essence, I learned to *earn* my students' respect. It was a revealing and painful metamorphic procedure to undergo, but it was well worth the discomfort it caused. I reached the point where I enjoyed teaching. I appreciated the students in a manner I could not before, and I appreciated their coming to me to "just talk." They hadn't done that before. Neither would I, had I been them. Who wants to talk to a tyrant?

Thus, I dropped the language and mask of the teaching stage, and I allowed the students and myself to enjoy the "real self" of each other. It was as though I were working in a different world, and I liked it!

The Tests and Trials of Today's Teachers

I spent 17 years of my adult working life as a classroom teacher, and some of my days were so pleasant, I thought I had the most gratifying career a person could have. Other days were so frustrating and fast-paced, I considered trading in my teaching credentials for certification in a lower stress job . . . perhaps lion taming! But perhaps such extremes are typical of most occupations.

Actually, when one stops to think about it, lions and teenagers do have a great deal in common. Both are perceived to be powerful, brave, and bold as they strive toward their goals. Lions and teens seem to share a sense of adventure and mystery, as those around them wonder what they are all about and what their next move will be.

Both appear to oscillate between profoundly frustrated restlessness and exceptionally peaceful contentment. Both are quite territorial and will defend their positions and possessions to the death. Both lions and teens generate a sense of superiority as they live up to their name of "King of the Jungle."

What motivates one to become an educator? Is it a desire to make a difference in a young person's life? Is it a sense of wonder at watching a student develop during a nine-month period of time? Is it a wish to simply be part of the learning process? Or is it all of the above?

For years I wondered if working with young people kept me young or made me old. I never did come to a definite conclusion. But the longer I considered the question, the more I concluded it was most likely a combination of both.

The everyday stress of dealing with teenagers and their difficulties definitely takes a toll on one's physical and mental health. I could not help but worry when one of the girls shared with me that she had been sexually molested the previous year. And I found myself burdened when one of the boys told me that he was quitting school to take a low-paying job that would allow him to help support his baby. When I reminded him that dropping out of school would be a foolish move because he would be less able to support his child in the future, I felt despair when he said, "But I have to think about **NOW**." I knew a vicious cycle was beginning and that everyone involved would be losers to some extent.

Yet seeing students overcome difficult hurdles brought a sense of satisfaction that, just perhaps, I played a part in their progress. Perhaps conversations I had with troubled students convinced them that life was not really as hopeless as they thought. Perhaps I helped them realize that they had options they had not considered, or that there definitely was a way out of their struggle.

When students were carrying a heavy burden and needed a listening ear, perhaps my advice (or silence) gave them the needed opportunity to sort out the dilemmas and find workable solutions within their own minds. On a more positive note, it was a delight to share in students' happiness and enthusiasm as they felt the excitement of new experiences.

I enjoyed hearing the boys talk about their first car as though they were brand new automobiles straight off the showroom floor. It didn't matter that they had invested in an older model that truly needed a paint job and tires. It didn't matter that their prized auto drank oil by the quart and guzzled gasoline by the gallon. What *was* important was that it was their car, and they were proud of it. And they wanted to tell me about them.

I took pleasure in having the girls tell me about their important date on Saturday night when their "special someone" surprised them with fresh flowers or a dinner at a nice restaurant where they could feel like real ladies. I appreciated seeing the smiles on their faces when they recounted their weekend activities, and they felt good about themselves. But I felt equally concerned when they sometimes shared the not-so-good things they experienced on their dates.

I wanted to somehow make them see the danger of their inclinations. I wanted to somehow protect them from an impending disaster I could see looming on the horizon. But all I could do was offer counsel. These things were part of their lives . . . and they had to live them!

Learning is a hard lesson for young people.

It is also a difficult time for the older folks in their lives as they stand by and see the inevitable coming full steam ahead.

It is especially hard for those older people who love those younger people!

At first glance, casual conversations between teachers and students may appear to be a waste of time and irrelevant to the learning process. But there is much more to it than that. Many students today come from homes where parents are too busy to take an active part in their teenagers' lives.

These students are hungry for someone to listen to them and share their daily activities and thoughts. There may be problems resolved during these conversations, but problem-solving should not be the goal. What *should* be of prime importance is the fact that a personal relationship is developing between the teacher and the student. By taking personal time with students, teachers are saying that they care about these students on a nonacademic level and that their private lives are also important. Students translate this attention to mean that they have a basic importance as human beings.

In addition to discussing automobiles, the boys in my class enjoyed talking about sports. It was not important that I understood the execution of a particular football maneuver or the workings of a Chevy 350 engine. What *was* important was that both teacher and student saw a special side of each other. In fact, students appreciate seeing a teacher's lack of knowledge in a particular area. I have seen students who are normally disinterested in their surroundings "come to life" at the opportunity to "teach the teacher."

One thing I am certain of is that working with teenagers keeps one honest. Teens may be many-faceted creatures, but one characteristic they all share is the ability to detect a fake . . . quickly and accurately. I have decided that, more than anything else, students wanted me to be honest with them. They didn't expect me to be perfect. They didn't expect me to have all the answers. What they *did* expect, and *demand*, was that I be sincere and straightforward with them. I found that students learned to accept and trust me when I said, "I don't know." They knew that sometimes I didn't know, but they were testing me to see if I was honest enough to admit my ignorance on a subject. And that honesty built further trust. Perhaps that's the basis of all teaching . . . **relationships!**

Another matter that students were concerned about was the issue of fairness. I found that teenagers are quite willing to accept regulations and restrictions if such expectations are required of everyone. Nothing makes students angrier than to see a double standard in operation when a teacher prohibits a particular action from one student, yet permits it from another when that student tries to pressure the teacher to "bend the rules" for him or her.

However, students do recognize the need for an occasional exception under extenuating circumstances. But it is the daily inconsistencies they cannot accept. Students feel insecure, and therefore resentful, in a situation such as this because they do not know the location of boundaries. As much as students will attempt to push a teacher to the limit, they want those very teachers to stand their ground. Teenagers want adults in their lives to be in charge, for that means *security.*

Regardless of what students attempt to convey, they know it takes more of a teacher's time, energy, and concern to "hold the line" than it does to allow students to do as they please. I once had a student say to me, "My folks don't care about me. They let me do anything I want." What a sad commentary on a teenager's view of adult authority and responsibility!

There were days when I wanted to gather up all my hurting students, take them home with me, give them the care and attention they needed and deserved, and watch the changes take place that I believed would occur. But there are so many students like that in schools today, no teacher's home would be large enough . . . a subdivision would have to be rented.

And now today's teachers are faced with a dilemma. The next time someone asks them what they do for a living, should they say,

> "I teach school"

> or

> "I tame lions"?

American Education: Who Are the Real Losers?

The month is August, and parents and students alike are preparing to return to school for yet another nine months in the classroom. This can be traumatic for both parties. Christian psychologist and counselor Dr. James Dobson has stated that "Our schools must have enough structure and discipline to *require* certain behavior from students because one of the purposes of education is to prepare our children for life."

Dobson continues along this train of thought with the observation that children must know how to work, get along with others, stay with a task until it is completed, and submit to authority in order to cope with the demands of modern day living.

Due to the drastic changes in American education within the last few years, many of today's teachers are leaving the classroom. They cite local, state, and federal restrictive guidelines as one of their major concerns (especially in light of the fact that an increased number of students cannot read and write under these guidelines).

Other concerns include *increased* rights for students and simultaneous *decreased* rights for teachers, lack of traditional behavior, increase in violence, attacks upon teachers, lessened parental concern and involvement, and widespread burnout among colleagues and superiors.

Many of the current educational programs are filled with procedures that have been proven failures in the past. These include such concepts as ungraded systems, peer tutoring, open classrooms, inventive spelling, and whole language reading programs.

The inventive spelling is one of the major concerns. In this program, teachers are taught to encourage students to spell words to the best of their ability. Teachers are not to openly correct students' spelling errors. The assumption is that kids will "figure it out" somewhere along the line.

In math classes, students are not being taught to memorize the times tables and other basic math essentials. Instead, students are being instructed to reason out *why* 5 x 5 = 25. In the more traditional educational setting of the past, we understood why we arrived at mathematical totals (that was part of the basic instruction), but we were also required to learn the basic numbers by memorization.

The national reading level of American young people has sunk to all-time lows within the last two generations, as today's school children are emerging from classrooms completely unprepared to face the vocabulary challenges within their world.

The phonics approach to reading has been discouraged in today's classrooms for several years, and dictionary use in the classrooms is not encouraged. The tried-and-true system of teaching reading competence according to the phonics approach has been replaced by what is commonly known as the "whole language system." In this system of instruction, the teachers are to saturate the classrooms with printed materials of all types (including books, charts, magazines, etc.). It is believed that as the children are surrounded with print, they will learn to read.

Teachers must have very specific skills to implement the whole language system, and many of them have not been given adequate instruction to do so. Many teachers are floundering in their task, realizing that they have been improperly prepared.

We must realize that children have the following three different vocabularies as they prepare for communication in today's society: a *reading vocabulary* which is very limited, a *speaking vocabulary* which is more extensive, and a *hearing vocabulary* which is the most extensive of the three. Obviously, if children are taught to properly sound out new words they encounter, they will usually recognize that word (and its meaning) without further assistance. In the whole language approach, children will usually say, "That word isn't on my list yet" when experiencing new vocabulary.

Many reasons have been cited for today's drastic decrease to children's reading competency, including the following:

→ the mainstreaming of students with special learning difficulties into regular classrooms, thereby forcing teachers to attempt to reach extreme levels of learning capabilities;

→ overly crowded classrooms, thereby forcing teachers to divide their individual attention to students beyond a productive level;

→ parents who are too busy to spend quality time with their children in activities such as reading;

→ parents who, because they also came through a deficient reading program in school, are nonreaders themselves;

→ children's popular activities of today that allow them to passively exist in their leisure time, such as watching television, rather than exploring their world through the pleasures and treasures of reading.

In spite of the continued use of the whole language program in today's schools, a recent study from Washington tells us that "the experts" have decided that phonics is the best approach to the teaching of reading. Teachers worth their salt have known this since the beginning of modern education.

Today's teachers are also being taught that it is not their responsibility to tell a child something is either right or wrong. The expected teacher's response is to ask the children what *they* think. But unless we set a standard and establish guidelines for children, how can we expect them to know and recognize boundaries?

We would never put our children in a swimming pool and *assume* they know how to swim. We never put our children behind the wheel of a car unless we *know* they understand how to operate an automobile. Yet we put them in a classroom and *assume* they will figure it out for themselves! Then we think we have the right to blame the kids when they find themselves in a bad situation and can't decide what to do! And these students are our future leaders? Does that thought cause you a lot of concern?

Our society has turned out a generation of students who have a mentality that says, "Blame the teacher. Blame the preacher. Blame society. But don't blame me. It's not my fault." We have raised a generation of young people who are masters at placing blame for their actions upon every conceivable element in their lives, except where the blame rightfully belongs . . . upon themselves. They will not accept the responsibility for their actions, but rather they point an accusing finger at anyone and everyone who might possibly serve as their scapegoat. And if a plausible excuse is not readily available, these individuals will create one!

Employers across the nation are begging for workers with a sense of responsibility, a good work ethic, and integrity. They are also begging for workers who can "think." Personnel in charge of placing high school seniors in work programs are hearing employers say repeatedly, "Today's young people cannot *think*. They have no cause-and-effect reasoning ability." A large portion of today's youth see no relation between today's labor and tomorrow's fruit.

Many of today's youth are consumed with demanding their **rights**. But they do not want to discuss their **responsibilities!** They see no connection between the two!

Yet in the midst of focusing upon these frightening negative conditions, we must remember that there are many good, productive young people who are making a valuable contribution to their family, their community, and their society. But, unfortunately, these students are becoming more and more in the minority.

There are many hard-working, conscientious, caring teachers from kindergarten through high school in today's classrooms. They are desperately concerned for today's young people. And many of these teachers are leaving their profession, for they feel they are fighting a losing battle. Those who are staying are experiencing unbelievable stress and frustration.

As this stress/frustration/lack of productivity cycle continues, everyone involved is a loser. Parents who truly care are desperately searching for a solution. Teachers who are genuinely concerned are begging for answers. And society, as a whole, is staggering under the weight of gross incompetence.

But who are the *real* losers in this nightmarish scenario? *THE STUDENTS* . . . those who cannot function at today's expected levels of performance. They are wondering what happened. And they are fearful of tomorrow. Or worse yet . . . *they don't care!*

It is time for us as family and friends of tomorrow's leaders to take a stand. It is time for us as a society and as a nation to take a stand. It is time to demand that our educational structure be returned to former, proven acceptable methods of instruction and levels of performance . . . levels at which children learned to spell, learned to read, learned to write, and learned to do the four basic math functions. It is time to eliminate the popular view that "society owes me."

It is time to return to the days when we taught our young people to **think** and **be accountable** for their behavior!

. . . about

WAR and PATRIOTISM

"The war that will end war will
not be fought with guns."
                              - *Anonymous*

Now He Belongs to the Ages

Each United States President has made his own unique contribution to American history, and our political inclinations decide whether we think those contributions have been favorable or unfortunate. Most Americans recall isolated facts relating to specific presidents, but the majority of people, when asked to quickly name one U.S. President, will only remember Abraham Lincoln.

Lincoln served as the 16th President of the United States from 1861-1865 during the dark days of the Civil War. He was the sole President to be born in Kentucky and died at the young age of 56. Only three other Presidents died at a younger age . . . James Polk (53), James Garfield (49), and John Kennedy (46).

Adults and children alike have the mental picture of Lincoln as the great lawyer, statesman, and orator delivering the famous Gettysburg Address. But if speakers are born and not made, Abraham Lincoln was not destined to be a speaker. He did not have many of the natural graces of an orator. After hearing Lincoln speak, one reporter observed, "He never knows where to put his hands and feet. They are always in his way."

Observers said that Lincoln's anatomy was composed mostly of bones, and when walking, his gangly gait resembled "the offspring of a happy marriage between a derrick and a windmill." Henry Clay and Daniel Webster, with their silver-toned voices, were considered the outstanding speakers of the era. Lincoln, on the other hand, had a high pitched voice with a nasal quality.

Everyone is familiar with the mental picture of young Abe stretched out before the fire in his hand-hewn log cabin, reading his beloved books. Since pencil and paper were not readily available, Lincoln began his *writing career* by using charcoal on the back of a shovel.

Even as a youngster, Lincoln displayed his enjoyment of public speaking. Townspeople would gather as Abe delighted them with his imitations of traveling preachers and politicians who had recently traveled through the area.

According to his own testimony, Lincoln attended school "by littles." Asked by reporters to estimate his total schooling, he replied that it would be less than one year. The formal education Lincoln received was in "blab schools" where all writing and reading were done aloud. He continued the habit of reading aloud while writing until his death.

However, this custom of reading aloud did nothing to help improve Lincoln's spelling or particular aspects of grammar. Subject-verb agreement was especially difficult for him, as he once told the House of Representatives in 1848 that "our candidate don't suit us." In responding to a heckler in 1856, Lincoln shouted, "That ain't true."

During his days as a lawyer, Lincoln impressed his colleagues with his ability to question witnesses. An associate once stated, "It is a rare gift with him. It is a power to compel a witness to disclose the whole truth."

His ability to present legal information was so profound, he could make all 12 jurors (many of whom were poorly educated) understand even the most detailed aspects of a case. Yet he could also argue a complex case in front of an astute judge.

Someone once observed that eloquence is more than the ability to say the right thing at the right time and in the right manner. "It is the ability to say the right thing, in the right manner, to the right people, at the right time, and in the right place." And because Lincoln had the instinctive ability to find just the right word for all occasions, people loved to hear him speak. Lincoln always spoke of issues in which he had great interest and conviction; he verbalized his thoughts in a powerful and persuasive manner.

He was an insightful man who had the ability to express himself clearly and with great force. With this invaluable gift of speaking, Lincoln persuaded millions of people to accept *his* views as *their* views.

Lincoln never spoke merely to hear his own voice. A fellow lawyer once said that "Lincoln never tells a joke for the joke's sake; they are like parables of old . . . lessons in wisdom." And yet Abe gained a reputation for his story-telling.

These stories were borne out of Lincoln's awareness of, and interest in, the world around him. They were stories that were witty and humorous, stories that made people laugh as they learned, stories that reinforced main points, and stories that made people want to be in Lincoln's presence.

And that's the story. A boy who came from such humble beginnings that he was often ridiculed by fellow classmates, a young man who began his speaking career standing on an empty keg, a lawyer who commanded respect from colleagues and adversaries, and a United States President who would be forever remembered for his honesty, his compassion, and his loyalty to what he knew was right and just. Lincoln would share his words of wisdom with all who would listen. He would share them with a renowned lawyer, a hard-nosed editor, a beloved family member, a child, or a stranger. And today, more than 130 years after his death, Abraham Lincoln shares his following words of wisdom with us:

— Stand with anyone who stands right. Stand with him while he is right, and part with him when he does wrong.

— The loss of enemies does not compensate for the loss of friends.

— Take hold of an honest heart and a strong hand. Do not let any questionable man control or influence you.

— Our defense is in the preservation of the spirit which prizes liberty as the heritage of all men, in all lands, everywhere.

Upon Lincoln's death, one gentleman observed that "Now he belongs to the ages." This wise individual realized that Abraham Lincoln, although he had physically lived during the 1800s, had transcended the time barrier with his memorable accomplishments, his intense love for his fellow man, and his deep appreciation for the human spirit.

World War II Begins

U.S DECLARES WAR ON JAPAN

England Joins In Clash Against Japanese

HAWAII SUFFERS HEAVILY FROM ATTACK

Those are the headlines from my hometown newspaper dated Monday, December 8, 1941, My mother, having been a writer herself, made a practice of saving papers and articles from special occasions. And I, at her death, had the privilege of sorting through these treasures and keeping those I desired.

I was not to be born until three and a half years after this paper was published, so I do not have personal recollections of the event, but I attempt to visualize how it must have been. The paper has, of course, yellowed with age. Yet its fourteen pages are in remarkably good condition. However, I still handle it with extreme care. I treasure this item because it is an historical document. But its more priceless value comes from the fact that it was my mother herself who handled it and tucked it safely away for my future use.

The three-cent northeastern Ohio newspaper tells me that the weather that day was to be "cloudy and continued rather cold with light snow tonight and tomorrow; brisk westerly winds."

An article released by The Associated Press informs readers that the U.S. Congress stood behind President Roosevelt's request and declared war on Japan through a senate vote of 82 to 0, and a house vote of 388 to 1. The only dissenting vote came from

Miss Jeanette Rankin, a Democratic congresswoman from Montana. She apparently had been among the few who also voted against the 1917 declaration of war on Germany. One must wonder the reason behind such a solitary vote.

The only front-page item *not* related to the war is a two-inch square box at the bottom of the page. Its contents show a Jack-in-the-box popping out and startling a surprised little fellow with a reminder that there were "14 Shopping Days till Christmas."

That strikes a bitter, ironic chord! At the top of the page, we are told that war has again broken out. That millions of families around the world will suffer. That hundreds of thousands will return from the battle in flag-draped coffins or in wheelchairs. That physical and emotional scars will remain for a lifetime. That property damage will be devastating. And that life on planet Earth will never again be the same as human battles human, soldier against soldier, and nation against nation.

But at the bottom of the page, we are reminded that the happy holidays of Christmas are just around the corner when presents will be purchased, gifts will be wrapped, family and friends will gather to celebrate cheer, hot meals will be enjoyed, and memories will be relived.

Yet what of the families whose husbands, fathers, sons, brothers, uncles, and nephews will be absent? Perhaps for this one Christmas. Perhaps for several. Perhaps forever. Can we hear the fear in their hearts, the prayer petitions in their souls for safety, and the questions in their minds?

Back in the paper, we see late-breaking war bulletins announcing that Churchill would broadcast to the world, British cruisers were reported sunk, Brazil was ready to give solidarity to the U.S., Haiti joined the war against Japan, Japanese aliens were seized by the U.S., and a U.S. transport was reported sunk.

Although articles relating to the war are throughout the paper, we are again reminded to shop for Christmas, with advertisements for the following **gift items for men:**

Knit scarf and glove sets	$1.50	to	$3.00
Handkerchiefs	.10	to	.50
Men's belts	.50	to	2.50
Smart luggage	11.50	to	35.00
Pajamas	1.65	to	4.95
Evans slippers	3.95		
Overcoats/Topcoats	19.95	to	40.00
Wool and leather jackets	7.50	to	21.00

And for the ladies:

Jumbo-knit cardigan	2.99		
Soft suede cloth dresses	1.99		
Silk hosiery	.59		
Luxury quilted robes	5.00	to	6.79
Rayon slips	.59		
Fur-trimmed Boucles [coats]	17.79		

And for the family:

G.E. "Blanket with a Brain" automatic heating blanket	37.95

From the local drug store, one could choose:

Evening in Paris gift set	2.00		
Coty Bath powder	1.00		
Gillette Tech Razor	.49		
Electric sandwich grilles	1.49		
Pipes	.50	to	1.50
14" Mama doll	.59		
14" Mama doll with long dress	.98		

From the local hardware store:

Union Hardware leather roller skates	7.95
Tubular ice skates	2.98

And from the town's largest furniture store:
a quarter-page ad featuring "A GIFT for HER to enjoy
for years . . . DEXTER . . . the gift of usefulness."
And what *was* this Dexter thriller? A washing
machine, of course:

> "Here's quality never before available in a
> washer at such low cost! Large wringer
> rolls, sturdily constructed, economical in
> operation, and easy to use, fully
> guaranteed! See it - - - compare it! **$79.95**
> * TRADE IN YOUR OLD WASHER *"

If the newspaper reader needed entertainment, one choice
movie was *SUNDOWN* starring Gene Tierney, with Bruce Cabot,
George Sanders, Harry Carey, Joseph Calleia, and Sir Cedric
Hardwicke.

Or perhaps the moviegoers would rather view *REMEMBER
THE NIGHT* with Barbara Stanwyck and Fred MacMurray. Or
perhaps *FATHER TAKES A WIFE* with Adolphe Menjou and
Gloria Swanson. Or how about *CADET GIRL* with Carole Landis
and George Montgomery.

In the obituary column, the deceased's name was given, along
with age, birth date, date and time of death — pretty much as we
are accustomed to today. However, in each case, the cause of
death was given in detail, along with the length of residency in
the area, birthplace, and names of all family members. In some
cases, friends were instructed to call at the home, rather than the
funeral home.

The classified section featured much the same ads as one sees
in today's papers except for the prices, of course.

And we must not forget the Comic Section. And there they are . . . at the top of the page . . . Blondie and Dagwood! Neither have aged a day. Dagwood is sitting in the same chair, next to the same table, reading his paper, with the same strands of hair sticking from his head. And he chased the neighbor boy from the house when Philip disturbed his reading time. Nothing has changed.

But the other strips contain unfamiliar titles: Polly and Her Pals, Tillie the Toiler, the Gumps, Tim Tyler's Luck, Toots and Casper, and Little Annie Rooney. And, needless to say, there is the crossword puzzle which no decent newspaper would omit from its "funnies" section.

A newspaper that typifies a day in history. A war begins that will alter the future of mankind, yet individuals are reminded to shop for Christmas, read installment-type stories, recognize those who have passed away, select their favorite movie, read the funnies, and work the crossword. The world stops. Yet the world moves on.

In looking back to that fateful day, we confirm President Roosevelt's prediction in that December 8, 1941 newspaper coverage that "yesterday was 'a date which will live in infamy.'"

World War II Ends

PEACE

Shooting Ends in Pacific

Another newspaper from my mother's treasure-house of keep-sakes. A companion to the paper dated December 8, 1941. But this one, dated Wednesday, August 15, 1945, brings news of PEACE. It is spelled out in 4-inch tall, red letters as it announces the glad tidings to the world.

The shooting ended in the Pacific, but would it ever end in the hearts and minds of those who witnessed the fighting? Would the questions and doubts ever cease to haunt the living victims of such atrocities? Would the dreams and nightmares ever cease, as soldiers and others involved attempted to reclaim a semblance of normal lives as civilians?

In celebration of Japan's unconditional surrender, the newspaper announced that all stores would be closed on that day. President Truman announced a two-day holiday for government workers and workers in general.

Also, the state's governor announced that the two days would be proclaimed as a holiday for "days of rejoicing for victory and days of prayer for the future." The governor added, "It is my earnest wish that the people of this state assemble in their respective places of worship at an appropriate hour to express grateful acknowledgment of divine favor and to pay tribute to those who brought us deliverance from the sufferings of war and establish the triumph of righteousness over tyranny and aggression."

Then there is the quarter-page drawing of the angel coming down from the heavens, carrying the olive branch, a sign of peace. As the throngs of people on earth raise their hands in joy and thanksgiving, attention is drawn to the banner flowing from the celestial being and the branch which proclaims, "PEACE." At the top of the drawing is the caption,

"Thank God!"

A special editorial titled "Victory in the Pacific" reminded readers that the victory in the Pacific had brought an end to the greatest and most costly conflict in the history of the world [to that point in time], and that perhaps for the first time in human history, a permanent PEACE had been put within the grasp of man. Such victory was a triumph of one way of life over another. It was an end to the tragic slaughter of human beings. It brought release from hated duties and rigors of war to millions of American men and women.

The editorial went on to state that we, as a nation, could not mistake either the victory or the peace as a final or enduring achievement. That the Pacific War had been won by American fighting men and machines and resourcefulness and spirit . . . and at the frightful cost of American lives and casualties. That it was American weakness in the Pacific that *CAUSED* the war. That we had allowed ourselves to become dangerously and almost suicidally weak in that area. That we had failed to acquire military, naval, and air bases necessary for the discouragement of the assault we knew Japan was planning against us.

In his report to the nation on the Potsdam Conference, President Truman pledged to "maintain our bases necessary for the complete protection of our interests and of world peace."

In a special Daily Pictorial Review, the paper displays photos of crowds around the U.S. waving flags, holding up newspaper headlines proclaiming victory, and strangers kissing strangers. Ticker tape, streamers, and beverage bottles are seen everywhere.

But even in the midst of rejoicing, individuals were called up short to account for their actions. In Pittsburgh, Pennsylvania, a man was charged with kicking a policeman during the height of a victory celebration.

From scanning the paper, the reader quickly sees the expected contents. Merchandise sales, sports events, comics, and (of course) the movies. Bette Davis was starring in *The Corn is Green,* while Greer Garson and Gregory Peck starred on the big screen in *The Valley of Decision.* For the more romantically inclined, the choice movie appeared to be *Thrill of a Romance*, with Van Johnson and Esther Williams.

But from the frivolity of movies, one's attention is quickly drawn to a half-page article by Earl Carroll, American business man who was thrust into the dangerous dual role of civilian leader and underground chief at Santo Tomas internment camp in Manilla. His coverage describes the brutal execution of three British prisoners who had tried to escape from Santo Tomas.

As Carroll continues his documentation, he tells of the brutal nature of many of the camp's officers. But he also describes acts of kindness from his enemies. Tomoyasu, the old camp commandant, had gone before his superiors in an attempt to stop the executions. He returned to Carroll, saying he had been unable to do anything as a Japanese officers, but that he would now "humble myself by removing my uniform and pleading before the authorities as an ordinary Japanese citizen." Tomoyasu was soon seen emerging from his quarters, wearing a kimono and wooden sandals. He climbed into his car and drove away. He returned an hour later, sending word to Carroll that he had failed again.

Carroll also recalls a time when a Japanese vessel arrived with the first American Red Cross shipment of supplies for the prisoners. When word reached the internees, they told Tomoyasu they wanted to see the manifest showing everything that had been sent to them because they were afraid his countrymen had stolen most of the shipment. As Tomoyasu went to the ship, he got the captain drunk and stole not one, but two, copies of the ship's manifest.

We tend to think of the suffering only from our perspective, yet what of the enemies' suffering. They, too, were husbands, fathers, sons, uncles, and nephews who loved and were loved. They, too, were prisoners of the Americans who, perhaps, suffered torture at *our* hands . . . something we find almost impossible to contemplate. We find it difficult to think of our men being brutalized by our enemies. But our minds cannot seem to absorb the possible reality of *our country* and *our men* doing the torturing.

There is the story from the International News Service of Japanese War Minister Korechika Anami committing suicide at his official residence to atone for his part in Japan's surrender. And what of the bomber shot down 35 minutes *after* the victory-signifying battle ensign was flown?

How tragically, how pathetically, how prophetically were the words written in that August 15, 1945, newspaper that " We have won a great war, but we have not assured ourselves AGAINST future wars of greater dangers to us, more exacting upon our resources of life and wealth, more gravely menacing to our free institutions and our national security and sovereignty."

As history records, World War II was said to be "the war that will end all wars."

How sad that it was not true.

How sad that more wars would follow.

That more lives would be lost.

That more families would be destroyed.

How Many Wars Will It Take?

I was born near the end of World War II, and I am certain that people around the globe were thinking they had lived through the war that would end all wars. But they were tragically and sorrowfully wrong. And I am wondering if we will *ever* see an end to war. I have been thinking a great deal about war lately and the devastating effect it has upon all concerned.

In April of 1917, our nation became involved in the fighting of World War I, the second-ranking most bloody and costly war in modern history. We had been declaring our neutrality for the three years of conflict prior to that date, but our involvement became mandatory when German acts of aggression (including the sinking of American merchant ships by German submarines) left our nation with no other option.

The brutality of this war left the United States with 320,518 military casualties (including 116,516 dead, 204,002 wounded, and 4,500 missing or prisoners of war).

On December 8, 1941, the U.S. entered World War II after the Japanese bombed Pearl Harbor the previous day. Again our nation had attempted to avoid the conflict for the previous 27 months (when Germany had invaded Poland), but the naval base attack left our nation with no alternative. This war still holds the grizzly distinction of being *the **most*** bloody and costly war in modern history. Reports tell us that our country spent 10 times as much money during this war as it had in all its previous wars combined.

Our nation suffered a devastating 1,215,954 military casualties in this nightmarish war (including 405,399 dead, 670,846 wounded, and 139,709 missing or prisoners of war.) Peace was declared on August 15, 1945, and I am certain that millions around the world thought that with the dropping of the first atomic bomb, peace had finally arrived.

But peace was not meant to be.

Our nation and our people again found themselves in battle during the Korean War from 1950-1953 after President Harry S. Truman ordered U.S. forces to help defend South Korea when the North Korean Communist troops invaded. This traumatic war cost our nation 162,708 casualties (including 54,246 dead, 103,284 wounded, and 5,178 missing or prisoners of war).

But perhaps the most tragic war in our history occurred between 1957-1975 as a battle for control of South Vietnam between the Communists and the anti-Communists dragged on for what seemed to be an eternity. We refer to this dark period in our history as the Vietnam War era. The U.S. began withdrawing its troops in 1969 and, as confirmed at that time, completed that withdrawal in March of 1973. Our country was *not* involved in the last 25 months of the battle, but that did little to ease the heartache of the American families who lost loved ones. This war devastated our country with 211,471 total casualties (including 58,167 dead; 153,303 wounded; and 2,207 *still* missing in action, with 1,621 believed to be in Vietnam). In a report issued by the Department of Defense, there are no listed statistics for total missing or prisoners of war.

In the name of professional accuracy, I must go back and correct something I said in the previous paragraph. Did you know that the Vietnam War was not a war? It was a "conflict," since **war** was never *officially* declared! Our bureaucrats in Washington do like to play their word games, don't they? It really is academic whether it was a *war* or a *conflict,* isn't it? The loss is the same. The pain is the same. The cost is the same.

This "fought in the jungle" war had far-reaching effects upon the United States of America. In all previous wars, all returning veterans were welcomed home as heroes. However, that was not the case in this conflict. Many Americans believed that our country had failed to achieve her goals. In addition, many American citizens felt our participation in this endeavor had been immoral and/or unwise. And because of the treatment many of our men received at the hands of their fellow citizens, many returning soldiers suffered from deep psychological wounds, high rates of divorce, drug abuse, and suicide. Many others were participants in violent crimes and were victims of joblessness.

The most recent battle involving U.S. troops is, of course, the Persian Gulf War which lasted from January 17 - February 28, 1991, when Iraq refused to leave Kuwait. Sources from the Department of Defense tell us that 148 individuals lost their lives in battle death, while 145 individuals died of non-battle wounds. This same source lists the wounded as 467. Again, as with the Vietnam War, there are no statistics for MIA's or POW's for the Persian Gulf War that I could locate.

By invading Kuwait, Saddam Hussein had hoped to increase Iraq's power within OPEC and acquire Kuwait's oil wealth (thereby eliminating the Iraqi debt to Kuwait). He also wanted a better access and more harbors into the Persian Gulf, plus keeping the Iraqi military busy in an attempt to end military attempts to force him out of power.

On the surface, it may appear that our nation *got off easy* in this latest conflict. Although Hussein was forced to leave Kuwait, one will recall that, as he left, his forces damaged and set fire to many of Kuwait's oil wells. In addition, he was responsible for dumping millions of gallons of crude oil into the Persian Gulf. Both of these acts resulted in untold damage to wildlife and the environment.

A new horror surfaced during Vietnam and the Persian Gulf that had not been used in this century since World War I. This horror will inevitably change the face of war forever. Chemical, biochemical, and radiological warfare were hurled upon mankind with devastating results that may carry into future generations. No longer will it be merely the soldiers in battle who suffer the damage, but their offspring (perhaps for generations to come) as genetic makeup may be altered. The gas, spray, powder, and liquid forms of the chemicals are responsible for injuries ranging from blisters . . . to blindness . . . to allergic reactions . . . to mental confusion . . . to cancer.

Sadly, such destructive contamination attacks not only human bodies. It devastates food supplies which, in turn, continues to destroy each individual who eats affected crops.

As much as we would like to boast that humankind is becoming more civilized, we cannot. Not considering the fact that we are not the first generation to use such horrifying tactics. The Spartans used such warfare during the Peloponnesian War in the 400s B.C. Ancient soldiers threw plague-infested bodies into food and water sources, thereby spreading the deadly disease. During the French and Indian War, blankets which had been used by smallpox victims were given to Indians in an attempt to destroy their people.

Totaling the above stated war statistics from just this century, we see that America has lost *at least* 1,910,651 men and women to war casualties (including 632,621 dead, 1,131,902 wounded, and 151,594 missing or prisoners of war). However, these are just numbers.

And numbers are cold, hard facts.

But the reality of war is that it is very personal, and many of the wounds *never* heal.

When we think of those who gave their lives, do we stop to consider that each person was a son or a daughter who never had the opportunity to return home and allow his or her parents to witness the growth into middle age.

Or a father who never saw his child that was born after he left? Or perhaps a father who never returned home to help raise his children? Or a brother/sister who never took part in a sibling's wedding? What of the mothers and the fathers and the wives and the husbands and the brothers and sisters who suddenly had to continue their lives with a giant empty void, wondering how they would ever cope? And what of other family members and friends who had to deal with their losses?

When we think of those who were wounded, do we consider that each injury represented pain and suffering, at best? Or do we try to imagine attempting to adjust to life with the loss of eyesight or missing limbs or scarring or severe psychological damage? Do we try to imagine the enduring of surgeries, therapies, and long hospital stays?

Can we imagine the terror of long-lasting nightmares in which the subconscious mind attempted to deal with war-related horrors?

What of the prisoners of war who suffered physical, emotion, and mental deprivation *and* torture beyond anything that some of us can imagine? How the indomitable spirit of the human will to survive was put to the ultimate test! And to realize that some of those prisoners who suffered the *most*, talk the *least* about it!

But perhaps the most tragic of all are the families of the MIA's . . . those families who have never been able to experience the closure that is so necessary in the grieving process. Have we ever stopped to consider living each day wondering if the person we loved were either living or dead? And if dead . . . was it swift and sure, or was there prolonged suffering? And if still alive . . . what torment they were experiencing or what isolation they were enduring?

Are these *pleasant* thoughts?

Of course not.

Are these *necessary* thoughts?

Absolutely!

For when we read of war and all that it involves, we must NEVER forget the real cost! Loss of humanity in so many forms!

How tragic.

And how sad.

How many wars will it take?

. . . about

HUMAN NATURE

"After all, there is but one race ---
humanity."

- Moore

Cranium Cleaning

Most of us are tidy-minded people. We spend time cleaning our basements, sorting through our attic treasures, washing our windows, dusting our furniture, vacuuming our carpets, bathing the dog, washing the car, and occasionally hosing down our driveways. We take time to rid ourselves of unwanted clutter. But what is *clutter*? It is a word we use in our daily vocabulary, yet take a moment before reading further and attempt to define it . . . . . .

The thesaurus lists *clutter* as "confusion, disarray, disorder, jumble, litter, mishmash." MISHMASH? Now that's a new word! I wonder if it has any connection to "Splish, splash, I was takin' a bath . . . "? There's that tidy-mindedness again! There doesn't seem to be any escaping the Cleaning/Sorting Syndrome. Except, perhaps, in one area of our lives.

How long has it been since we participated in some good old "Cranium Cleaning"? We attempt to keep the dirt and junk from all the other areas of our life . . . but what about the confusion, disarray, disorder, jumble, litter, and mishmash that occurs in our head? Do we take care of that part of our lives, or do we feel that our thoughts just go along for the ride?

In Scripture, Proverbs 23:7 tells us that "whatsoever a man [woman or child] thinketh, so is he [she]." In other words, our thoughts control the entire remainder of our lives. Our actions, our motives, our feelings, everything. Quite a sobering thought, I'd say! We are concerned about the dust balls in our homes, but are they as important as what makes us what we are? What about the dust balls in our *brains*? If our thoughts control who we are, should we not spend extra time keeping that part of our life in order?

We often excuse our thoughts with "That's just the way I am" or "I had a tough childhood" or "You just don't understand." We offer such poor excuses for our thoughts because we are often too angry or afraid to face the real issues that lurk inside our skulls and our hearts. We somehow think we should not be held accountable for what we think. After all, it must be our parents' fault, our teachers' fault, our preacher's fault, or society's fault. But *our* fault? *NEVER!*

If you are not willing to accept proper responsibility for your thoughts, please do not read any further. It will be a waste of your time. But if you are ready to take part in some cranium cleaning, please continue.

Let's first begin our cleaning by starting at the beginning. That's always a good place to start. For one full day, be consciously aware of whether your thoughts are positive or negative. Is your glass half full or half empty? Are you enjoying today's beautiful weather, or are you dreading the not-so-beautiful weather that is being predicted for the day after tomorrow? Are you basically an upbeat or downbeat person?

If you are in the negative and pessimistic category, make an honest effort to turn your thought patterns around. It may be difficult, and it may take some time. After all, we *are* creatures of habit. But this task can be accomplished with some personal determination and effort.

Second, scrounge around the corner of your mind for those long-hidden thoughts of anger or resentment either toward people in your past or your present. Whether or not these thoughts are justified, ask yourself what purpose they are serving and who is being hurt the most by their presence. If they are not helpful or productive, why continue allowing them to take up precious time and space? Each time a negative thought about a person comes to mind, make a conscious choice to think of something *good* about that individual. Again, it may take some time, but it will be worth the effort to yourself and to those individuals with whom you must live. For if we are harboring a lot of negative feelings, we are not very nice folks to be around. In fact, most people will go out of their way to avoid us!

Third, begin searching for evidence of jealous thoughts. We know we are not supposed to entertain jealousy, but we often do. We so envy other people, their situations, or their possessions that we cannot enjoy the blessings we have. We must choose whether *we own our possessions* or whether *our possessions own us!* We must decide whether we will be the master or the slave. Again it becomes a matter of CHOICE.

Last, we must explore our thoughts for boredom and dissatisfaction. Such thoughts are extremely dangerous, for they may lead to depression and stagnation. We become overwhelmed with despair and gloom as this vicious cycle continues, and we become more miserable with each passing day.

Have fun with life! Explore new things! Try new ideas! Let the adventuresome part of you take control for a while and do something you've always wanted to attempt! It may be visiting a particular vacation spot. It may be taking up a new hobby. It may be joining a new sports team or local gym. It may be furthering your education or becoming involved in a worthwhile cause.

Your cranium cleaning process may be in making a damaged relationship right again by offering or accepting an apology. Give yourself a wonderful gift today, and exercise the courage to do what you know you should.

There used to be an old custom of having a murderer carry his victim strapped to his back. As the corpse continued to decay, the guilty party became a victim himself as he endured the weight and the stench of the rotting body. There is a real lesson to be learned here, and it is that we must rid ourselves of garbage in our lives. If we do not, we will become its victim. And we do not want to continue through life carrying such a dreadful load.

But whatever it is,

    TRY IT!

        You may not be successful in your first attempt.

           And then, again, you may be.

But either way, you have had the courage and fun of giving it your best shot. And there is tremendous satisfaction in that!

One's Inner Self:

Part I

During the 1970s, University of California football coach John McKay was interviewed on television. One of the topics of discussion was his son's athletic ability. John Junior was a successful player on his dad's team, and Coach McKay was asked to comment on the pride he felt over his son's accomplishments on the field.

His answer was very impressive and said a great deal about this father and son relationship. The coach stated that he was extremely pleased with John Junior's good season that year. McKay went on to elaborate that although his son did a fine job and he *was* proud of him, he would be just as proud of his son if he *never* played football at all.

Coach McKay was saying, in effect, that John's football talent was recognized and appreciated, but that his value as a son and as a human being did not depend upon his ability to excel in sports. Thus, his son would not lose his father's respect if the next season brought disappointment or failure. John's place in his father's heart was safely rooted in his inherent value of who he was, not upon how well he performed. It would be wonderful if every child could say the same.

To the contrary, human worth in our society is all too frequently reserved for those who "meet the standards." Physically attractive people are born with it. Highly intelligent individuals are likely to find approval. Superstar athletes are usually respected. But few people are considered valuable just because they *are*! Social acceptance is awarded very carefully, certainly excluding those who "do not qualify."

Keeping in mind the unconditional love and acceptance felt by John (Junior) McKay, let us consider the parent-child relationship of another young man. He began his life in New Orleans with all the classic handicaps and disadvantages. His mother was a powerfully built, dominating woman who found it difficult to love anyone. She had been married three times, and her second husband divorced her because she beat him up regularly. The young man's father died of a heart attack a few months before his birth and, as a consequence, his mother had to work long hours from his earliest childhood.

The mother gave her son no affection, no love, no discipline, and no training during those early years. She even forbade him to call her at work. Other children had little to do with him, so he was alone most of the time. He was poor and untrained and unlovable. When he was thirteen years old, a school psychologist commented that he probably didn't even know the meaning of the word "love."

Despite a high IQ, he failed academically and finally dropped out during his third year of high school. He thought he might find acceptance in the Marine Corps, but his problems went with him. The other marines laughed at him and ridiculed him. He fought back, resisted authority, and was court-martialed. He was also thrown out of the Marine Corps with a hardship discharge and $1500 in saved-up pay.

While in active duty, he scored two points above the minimum score requirement as sharpshooter. He was small and scrawny in nature, and he had an adolescent squeak in his voice. He was balding, had no talent, no skill, and no sense of worthiness. He didn't even have a driver's license.

Again he thought he could run from his problems, so he went to live in a foreign country and applied for citizenship. But he was rejected there, too. Although he was denied citizenship, he worked hard as a factory metalworker.

After returning to the United States, he is said to have threatened the life of a public official. Although he found work, his jobs were few. They never lasted long, and the pay was very low. He was described as "lonely," "brooding," and "tormented."

Shortly after he married, his wife left him, and he literally begged her to take him back. He relinquished all pride. He finally crawled. He accepted humiliation. Despite his meager salary, he brought his wife twenty-seven dollars as a gift, asking her to spend it any way she wished. But she laughed at him and belittled his attempt to supply the family's needs. She complained about the family's lack of money and her husband's "big ideas." She ridiculed his failure and made fun of his impotency in front of a friend.

No one wanted him.

No one had *ever* wanted him.

His behavior demonstrated a capacity to act quickly without considering the consequences. He seemed alienated from the world in which he lived. His life was one of isolation, frustration, and failure. He was inwardly and outwardly hostile, and he wanted to have a "place in history."

The next day, he was a strangely different man. He arose especially early, went to the garage, and took down an Italian rifle he had hidden there. That rifle was later traced to the young man through a Chicago mail-order firm. He carried it to his newly acquired job.

Who was this young man who lived such a tormented life? Who is this pitiful being whose childhood and adolescence molded and shaped his adulthood? In part II, we will discuss his identity, how his outward behavior mirrored his inner misery, and how his actions perhaps changed the course of history.

One's Inner Self:
Part II

The young man who lived such a tormented life, the pitiful being whose childhood and adolescence molded and shaped his adulthood was the infamous Lee Harvey Oswald. And from a window on the third floor of a book depository, shortly after noon that day, he allegedly fired two shells into the head of President John F. Kennedy.

Lee Harvey Oswald, the rejected and unlovable failure, allegedly killed the man many people believed represented all the success, fame, wealth, and family closeness that he, himself, lacked. John and Jackie Kennedy brought such a sense of beauty and romance to Washington that it was often referred to as Camelot.

Oswald's personal problems do not excuse his violent behavior, yet an understanding of his inner torment and confusion that began in childhood helps one to see him not only as a vicious assassin, but also as the pitiful, broken man he became.

He experienced the crushing awareness of his own inferiority and, as it often does, his grief turned to anger. Lee Harvey Oswald's inner child of the past destroyed his present *and* his future . . . and the future of those with whom he lived.

How can we, as parents and loved ones, build a strong sense of self-worth and indomitable spirits in our children, despite social forces that work against us? Numerous child psychologists and counselors offer several strategies that focus on early home life, the school years, the adolescent experiences, and matters relating to adults. If put into practice, these strategies will strengthen and encourage the inner child of the past so the future can be built upon . . . not destroyed.

Strategy 1. Observe the Educational Environment.
A parent must understand the difference between a child who *refuses* to work and a child who is *unable* to do required work. If academic problems arise, a proper diagnosis is essential through whatever means is necessary. This approach would include a physical, mental, and/or psychological evaluation by a person whose expertise within the specific field is acknowledged within the community. But this diagnostic process must be handled carefully so the child is not taught to rely upon unjustified excuses for difficulty. There is a vast difference between legitimate obstacles and convenient stumbling blocks.

Strategy 2. Teach Your Child "Positive Speech" Power.
Children must be taught the power of words at an early age . . . that words have the power to either hurt or heal. It must be emphasized that the words we hear from others play a vital role in our self esteem, but we must also teach the potency of the words we speak to *ourselves.*

Therefore, children must learn that demeaning, negative speech is habit-forming and that it accomplishes nothing constructive. Also remind children that this Positive Speech Power should also apply to other people and that individuals never make themselves look better by tearing others down.

Strategy 3. Discipline, Don't Punish.

There is a vast difference between discipline and abuse, and child abuse should never be tolerated by individuals or society. But as children deliberately step across the line of acceptable behavior, they must be disciplined in a positive manner that will lend itself to nurturing and instruction. Punishment, on the other hand, is a negative response which is directed at the child rather than the behavior. Children want a parental response when they have misbehaved. When there is no such response, a child sees it as neutrality on the part of the parent. As children are screaming, "Let me do my own thing," they are wanting care-givers to care enough to say *no*.

An old adage that "Sticks and stones may break my bones, but names will never hurt me" is a lie. And we must remember that in dealing with children. When correcting or disciplining, call attention to the acts . . . not the children Attempt to word all correction in a positive manner, and refrain from name-calling. If we, as adults, were to be corrected, would we rather hear, "You could have chosen a better alternative to the problem that would have saved you a great deal of time, such as . . ." (and then offer an alternative action). Or would we like to be the recipient of "I can't believe you were so stupid to waste all that time"?

We must always remember that words *do* hurt. They hurt a great deal. And they can leave a lifelong impression. We must never forget that our goal is to stop the behavior, not scar the child.

Strategy 4. Teach Character Values.
A parent is obligated to help a child compete in the world the best way possible. As much as is financially feasible, physical, emotional, or mental difficulties should be dealt with. Competition in sports or academics should stress that a small fraction of persons win consistently, and that losing may teach a person to be gracious in the face of defeat. This will be accomplished much more easily if earlier emphasis has been placed on what children *are* rather than what they *do*. Compliment children on their good qualities and characteristics, rather than always on their accomplishments and appearance.

Strategy 5. Save Teen Years for Teens.
The toy industry has dramatically changed the whole concept of children's play. Whereas yesterday's children playfully engaged in puppet shows, played "catch", and pretended to be mommies and truck drivers, they are now striving to live a lifestyle beyond their years and maturity level. Two of the most influential forces behind this trend have been body-beautiful dolls with Hollywood wardrobes, along with gory and violence-promoting trading cards and toys.

In addition to their toys, we permit our children to watch "fun" television that is filled with violence and fantasies. Fun-time cartoons are no longer fun, as constantly striving for the unattainable is stressed . . . as the leading characters are repeatedly placed in situations of increased threat . . . as the dark forces of evil are perpetually engaged in warfare. All of these "cliff hanger, life-and-death" episodes leave their young viewers with internal questions, concerns, and anxieties. We must remember that childhood should be a time of fun and enjoyment, not a time for little shoulders to carry big fears and worries.

Strategy 6. Evaluate Family Values.

From the time we were children, we have heard and seen external appearance and internal intelligence stressed as being highly sought-after qualities that are *necessary* for success. Yet we, as average parents, somehow believe that we have the responsibility or right to produce children that will one day astound the world with remarkable feats of accomplishment.

We, as parents, must always remember that we do not have the right to re-live our own lives through the lives of our children. Our own missed goals and opportunities must not be thrust upon our children as we attempt to re-capture the past. Our own mistakes of the past must not be a motivating force that moves our children into their future.

Strategy 7. Teach the Art of Compensation.

Some children seem to be born with the proverbial silver spoon in their mouths, while other children appear on the scene with three strikes against them. But parents can help a less-than-normal (whatever "normal" is) child realize that life is not always fair and that there are no simple cures. Parents must walk that fine line of distinction between allowing their child to be strengthened by adversity while protecting their child's spirit from being crushed in the process.

Strategy 8. Prepare Your Child for Change.
The primary reason adolescence is so distressing is because the young people do not fully understand what is happening to them. Many of their fears, anxieties, and discouragements could be lessened or eliminated by discussions and explanations. If the adolescent is to view the trials of a particular age as a temporary phase through which everyone must pass, distress is more tolerable. It is advisable to stress that adolescence is an age of dramatic physical, emotional, mental, psychological, and spiritual change.

Emphasize that feelings of inferiority, wanting to conform, an onslaught of confusion, and the trauma of identity crisis are normal and to be expected. Also explain that fluctuating emotions, sexual fascination, and the mixed *desire* and *fear* of increasing independence is a part of the growing process all living humans experience.

The formation of the inner child of the past (for which parents are primarily responsible) will be the most determining factor that will influence that individual's capacity to function within the adult world.

It is undeniably true that we are products of our environments. But that cannot excuse our adult behaviors. If our environment produced hurtful results within our own lives, we do have the *opportunity* and the *responsibility* to change that. For if we do not take charge of our future, we will continue in our learned patterns of behavior and will continue to hurt those around us as *we* were hurt.

Physical abuse is tragic, but the physical injuries heal. It is the emotional and psychological trauma that carries such lingering effects. Individuals often think they can heal themselves simply by refusing to discuss the incidents or to "just forget" them.

But psychologists and psychiatrists tell us that such hurt is never simply *forgotten*. Unless properly recognized and dealt with, accumulated trauma lies below the surface doing the work of an ugly cancer as it spreads its deadly effects. Such repressed, intense feelings will ultimately surface as physical ailments, emotional instability, depression, violent acts of aggression, or suicide.

We may think we cannot afford to seek professional help, either for reasons of finances or pride. But when we realize the ultimate consequences, can we afford *not* to seek appropriate help?

If Lee Harvey Oswald had been raised in a different home atmosphere by a different type of parent, how would his life possibly have been different? And if his life had been different, how would our world be different since November 22, 1963, in Dallas, Texas?

Personal Homicide

We have all heard it. We have all taken part in it. And most of us have been the victims of it. We hear a juicy tidbit about an individual, and we cannot wait to pass it on. The information may be true. It may be false. Sometimes we *know* which it is. Sometimes we *assume*.

But either way, we anxiously await, or sometimes *create*, the first opportunity to inform our acquaintances of our newly found information. After all, is it not our civic duty to permit our community to be current on all late-breaking news? Do we not owe it to our fellow humans to make them aware of any possible threat to their safety? If our information does not truly create a threat, then perhaps we should not repeat it.

However, due to our concern over humankind's tendency to have weaknesses, we must apprise our family and friends of these weaknesses so that all of us may be *prepared*. Prepared for *what*? To help that poor individual see and voluntarily correct the fault? And if the pathetic soul is already aware of the problem, perhaps our pressure and comments will bring sufficient shame to *force* the person to change! Or is that possible?

And, heaven forbid, if our information is not true . . . then what? We satisfy ourselves with the customary excuse that, after all, everyone makes mistakes. And besides, we are going to share our tidbit with just one or two others. Well, perhaps three. But even if it is four, that is really not such a large number, considering the number of acquaintances all of us have. Taking that into account, how much damage could we really do?

What truly makes this whole process acceptable, in the final analysis, is the widely known fact that *everyone* gossips . . . it is simply a way of life. No one, or hardly anyone, means true harm by their actions. It is a habit, and nearly every human being has been on either the giving or the receiving end of this indulgence. The most tragic aspect of this scenario is the untold hurt and damage inflicted upon the victim. Hurt and trauma that are beyond measure.

However, I have noticed something very interesting about gossip. Perhaps you have noticed it also . . . it is rarely positive. Why is that? What does it say about our human nature? I believe it says several things.

First of all, spreading negative gossip comes more naturally than positive compliments and reinforcement. Perhaps it comes more naturally because we *look* for faults more naturally.

Second, individuals are more *interested* in others' faults than they are in their strengths, and they would rather concentrate upon those faults. This makes for more interesting conversation.

Third, we attempt to mask our own inadequacies by focusing upon those of others. We somehow feel that if we can lessen the image of another, we will elevate ourselves. But what about the cost of such elevation? When we are alone with our thoughts . . . not out to impress anyone . . . how do we feel knowing that we use other people as rungs in our climb to the top of the image ladder?

Do we ever stop to consider the cost of such negative and damaging behavior? The cost to others and to *ourselves*? As we focus upon the negative aspects in the world around us, we become more negative ourselves. And as we become more negative, others tend to keep their distance from us, for no one wants to be near such a person.

As our isolation grows, we experience frustration and self doubt; our self-esteem begins to suffer. We compensate by falling into our expected mode of behavior . . . faultfinding! The ugly snowball has begun its downhill roll, and the longer it continues, the more speed it will gather, and the harder it will be to stop.

We have two choices. We can either continue in our past behavior, or we can determine within ourselves to stop (although it may be difficult) and begin to build people up rather than tear them down.

What if we choose to make amends for the damage we have caused?

For many years, there lived a man who had taken great pleasure in spreading scandalous stories (both true and untrue) about the people he knew. One day, he became the object of a vicious story; suddenly he became acutely aware of the damage he had inflicted upon others with his tales.

The man went to the elderly village leader who was known for his wisdom and good judgment, and he asked the old gentleman what he could do to repair all the damage he had done. In his realization of how many people he had hurt, he wanted to take back the stories he had spread.

The wise old man answered his request by saying, "Catch a wild goose. Then strip it of its feathers and scatter them to the wind. Then collect every feather!"

The talebearer responded, "But, Sir, I cannot possibly do that. The feathers could never be recovered!"

After a moment of silence that seemed to last an eternity, the wise old man replied, "Neither can you call back the stories you have spread. Neither can you undo the harm you have caused."

It is never too late to change our behavior.

But it *can* be too late to undo the harm we have caused!

Grandpap's Wisdom

Several years ago, I was talking to my grandfather concerning many different matters. You know how it is when grandfathers and granddaughters talk . . . skipping from the past to the present to the future and back to the past again. I can't really recall my thoughts leading up to my next question, but I remember myself asking, "Grandpap, how old do you have to be before people stop telling you what to do?"

His response both started and amused me. He looked me straight in the eye (there was nothing backward about Grandpap), and he replied, "I don't know, honey. I haven't gotten there yet. I'm only 95 years old. Your grandmother, your mother, and your Aunt Dee are *still* telling me what to do." We both laughed at his response, and then I began thinking seriously about its message.

In my early teens (goodness, that seems like a long time ago), I decided that 16 was the magical age at which everything would come under my domain. I would be driving myself around town, rather than being chauffeured by my parents. And the world would be wonderfully mine. However, I discovered that the police officers with their radar guns were controlling a large portion of what I did and did *not* do. The neighbors were also quite good at keeping my parents "informed" about my driving habits.

I changed my mind and decided that 18 must be the special age of getting to *do your own thing*. By that time, however, I was facing high school graduation, and the local board of education and the Ohio Revised Code were telling me what I would and wouldn't do in order to qualify for graduation.

Then I decided that 21 was the wonderful age of independence. But by that time I was still in college, and I had *professors* telling me what to do. In addition to that, the U.S. government was controlling a large portion of my life. The Vietnam War was at its peak, and dear old Uncle Sam was dictating when I could and could not set my wedding date . . . especially if I wanted my husband-to-be present at the ceremony. Since I was not criminally inclined, I had never *thought* of the government intervening in my affairs . . . especially something as important as my wedding!

The hoped-for age must be 25! Again I was disappointed. At that stage of my life, my husband was attempting to tell me what to do (although that didn't work so well). Neither of us had learned at that stage in our marriage that we both were grown adults, each with our own distinct views and ways of doing things. Both of us were willing to begin changing for the sake of matrimonial peace, but neither of us took too well to being *told* what to do. Fortunately, since that time, both of us have mellowed a great deal.

Furthermore, my employer was telling me what was expected. Had I missed something somewhere along the line, or was reality just beginning to register? Grandpap's words kept coming back to me with more frequency and intensity. Within a short time, the children began arriving, and *they* tried telling me what to do. That worked even less than my husband attempting to tell me what to do.

My dream was shattered! I was 30 years old, and people were *still* bossing me around. Would it never end? And, of course, society was laying its rules and regulations before me as it insisted on regulating my behavior.

And then the wisdom of Grandpap's comment dawned upon me! I must be a slow learner, for the comment's insight did not register with me for quite some time.

The mysterious age at which we no longer have others tell us what to do?

It doesn't exist . . . except in our dreams. We will always be compelled to abide by others' expectations to some degree, along with the law of the land. And there is more responsibility for those of us who possess moral and religious convictions. Not being able to do as we please may not seem fair at times, but think for just a moment of what would occur if each of us had our dreamed-for independence.

If we could do whatever we chose, whenever we wanted, and however we chose to do it . . . oh, what chaos! We would be immediate victims of anarchy whereby each individual would abide only by his or her own self-governing laws. No one would be accountable to anyone! I could do as I pleased. You could do as you pleased. Everyone could.

Suddenly our dream becomes a nightmare! The name of the game would be disorder, turmoil, mob rule, and lawlessness. None of us would be safe, and we would beg for governing regulations that would bring law and order to our lives. We would want a sense of safety and security restored.

When we watch human nature and compares it with animal behavior, we must admit that humans are often more vicious than their animal counterparts. Our carnal nature is to think of ourselves first, and to consider only that which will benefit Number One. We turn on our own offspring and abandon them in pursuit of our own interests. We abuse them in an attempt to deal with our own frustrations, and we even kill them in fits of anger. But the television advertisements constantly tell me to "Go on. Indulge. You're worth it."

When confronted with difficulty, we are quick to assert our *rights,* but we oftentimes have difficulty accepting our *responsibilities.* In spite of advanced medical knowledge and scientific advances in recent years, we continue to abuse ourselves with drugs, alcohol, tobacco, and excessive eating. Yet we, creatures of such self-destructive weaknesses, think we have the ability to reach a stage of life where we should be able to do as we please.

But fortunately, the ignorance of youth gives way to the wisdom of age . . . *usually*. And we realize that we can *never* be self-contained, unrestrained living organisms. And I, in my youthful ignorance, learned a great lesson from Grandpap, an insightful elderly man who had lived nearly a century.

During those nine and a half decades, Grandpap had seen many changes.

Changes in medicine.

Changes in education.

Changes in business.

Changes in science.

But in one area, Grandpap had seen no changes. He had seen no change in basic human nature. And he realized that we NEVER reach the point where we can do as we please.

Yes, But . . .

Have you ever looked at some undesirable characteristic in your personality, realize it came from your past, and wonder why you continued to behave in that manner as an adult? Have you ever wondered how that particular behavior has affected your own children? I didn't for a long time. Then something happened . . . something was said . . . that forced me to face reality.

It wasn't pleasant.

It wasn't easy.

But it was life-changing!

It was not until a very few years ago that I realized how my drive for perfection had its roots in my childhood. I also did not realize the effect it was having upon my own children. Since this revelation, I have tried very hard to change myself in this respect. But I have found the truth in the statement that "Old habits die hard."

It is true that I often felt superior to others, sought areas of involvement which would yield easily measured performance, and was considered very successful by those around me. After all, I had high quality results to show for my efforts!

At first, it was hard to understand how the effects of our inner child of the past affects our adulthood until one comes to the realization that those early stimuli and responses are so deeply ingrained into our being that we are unconscious of them. Yet the influence they have over us is so powerful!

Another vital realization has surfaced within the last few years that having only *one* parent who approves of us on the basis of performance can offset or deeply diminish the positive input being given by the other parent who does *not* operate within that mode. My mother, I knew, accepted me for who I was rather than what I did. I also knew that her love was unconditional. However, my father's attitudes and actions were extremely counterproductive to her efforts, although I did not realize it at the time. He showed approval when I did well at a task. When I didn't, he wasn't happy. I can't recall *how* or *when* I realized this, but, obviously, I got the message. Loud and clear.

Do well, get praised!

Do poorly, get fussed at or ignored!

It was not until a few years ago, during a conversation with my daughter, that I realized how I was carrying over my perfectionism into the lives of my own two children. Sarah had just completed a school project and had shown it to me for my response. I looked it over and said, "Very nice job. You really did well."

She looked at me and said, "Yes, but . . . "

I asked her what she meant, and she replied, "Well, you always tell me what a good job I have done, and then you proceed to tell me everything that's wrong with it and how to make it better."

Her comment hit me like a ton of bricks as I suddenly realized that my behavior was a flashback into my own childhood. I was doing to my children what had been done to me! And in that moment, I resolved to break the hideous cycle that can ruin generation after generation of innocent children.

It has been very difficult at times to change a whole lifetime of "programming," but with the help of an insightful husband, the situation has marvelously improved. Imagine, the catalyst was a comment from a twelve-year-old child! How true is the verse of scripture that says, "And a little child shall lead them."

Recognizing and dealing with the way my father had treated me took me through stages of bitterness, hurt, neutrality toward him, and finally acceptance. I came to realize that he, having been brought up in his type of home, was just as much a victim of environment as he had made me. He was raising me the only way he knew . . . the way *he* had been raised.

While we must accept that we are truly products of our environment, we must never use that as an excuse to continue unacceptable or poor behavior. We cannot always control the manner in which others treat *us,* but we can control the manner in which we treat *others.* It may take extreme determination, months or years of practice, and even professional intervention. But the choice is ours, and we must accept responsibility for that choice!

Several months later, I was grateful that as my father and I were approaching his upcoming death, I could accept him for what he was. There were no warm, loving fuzzies toward him. There was no deep love. He had destroyed that years ago, and I could not create something that did not exist.

But I *could* show respect for the fact that he was my father and that he was a human being who was fearing the future and perhaps regretting the past. Treating him properly was made easier by the realization that he did not influence me and raise me in the manner in which he did to be malicious. He did it as a result of being controlled by his *own* inner child of the past. His father had treated him as he had treated me.

And then, as the inevitable drew nearer, I did all I could to make his last days as pleasant as possible. However, the greatest relief and pleasure I experienced was in knowing that I was doing my deeds of kindness out of genuine concern for him . . . *not* out of a sense of guilt or approval-seeking.

That gave me the freedom to move on with my life.

The chain of generational behavior had been broken.

Amazingly, it had begun with the comment from a twelve-year-old.

Are you struggling with an undesirable behavior that began in your childhood? If so, are you willing to take the first step toward breaking that family tradition? If not, the negative consequences will continue to hurt and haunt those around you.

But if you are ready to put your inner child of the past behind you and move toward a more positive and fruitful future, take the following 4 steps:

Confide in someone you can trust and in whom you have confidence. Tell that individual of your negative behavior *and* of your desire to change. Ask him or her to positively support you and call it to your attention whenever you fall into that old behavior pattern.

Upon being reminded of your "slip," go to any individuals you may have hurt. Apologize. This will accomplish two things. First, it will confirm to the individual that you are truly attempting to change your behavior. Second, it will make you think twice before "slipping" again. After all, we don't enjoy apologizing, do we?

When you do stumble in your efforts, remind yourself that changing a long-held pattern of behavior is extremely difficult, and backsliding is *not* a cause for giving up. It may be an *excuse*, but never a *good reason*.

When you do well in your endeavor, give yourself a word of praise and a pat on the back. You have begun a difficult assignment, and you deserve a note of celebration. If the persons with whom you are dealing are also aware of your efforts, ask them if they, too, are aware of your accomplishment. There is certainly nothing wrong in asking for a little positive reinforcement.

The final choice is yours and yours alone. Do you want to be a slave to your past? Or do you want to break those chains and become the master of your future?

In deciding, remember . . .

> *You are free*
> to make choices.
> You are **not** free
> to escape the *consequences*
> of those choices!

. . . about

DEATH and GRIEF

"When death comes to me, it will find
me busy, unless I am asleep."
- Girard

Getting Past Pain and Pleasure

In the majority of our relationships, we never extend ourselves beyond the pleasure. We take satisfaction and experience joy at pleasure's presence, both in our own lives and the lives of those for whom we care. As we experience the good things of life, we desire to share that pleasure with those around us . . . whether those *good things* be material or nonmaterial.

As we appreciate the mountain-top experiences, we desire to have those around us feel the uplifting benefit. As we explore the unexpected blessings of our existence, we desire to share the abundance of such advantages. When we relish in the enchantment of our world, we want to extend that thrill to all who will take part. When we gather the surprise profits of our being, we want to spread their worth to those around us.

We want to *share,* and *share in*, the gratification and entertainment of life's pleasurable spices. Yet in nature, there is always a balanced counterpart. For day, there is night. For hot, there is cold. For wealth, there is poverty. For youth, there is age.

And for pleasure . . . there is pain.

Oscar Wilde, the Irish author and playwright who lived during the latter half of the 1800s, wrote that

"If a friend of mine . . . gave a feast, and did not invite me to it, I would not mind a bit . . . But if . . . a friend of mine had a sorrow and refused to allow me to share it, I would feel it most bitterly. If he shut the doors of the house of mourning against me, I would move back again and again and beg to be admitted, so that I might share in what I was entitled to share. If he thought me unworthy to weep with him, I should feel it as the greatest humiliation . . . ."

Who among us can share Mr. Wilde's thoughts?

Who among us can desire to partake in another's suffering?

Very few, I would imagine.

And why is that, do you suppose?

Is it that we feel uncomfortable with loss? Is it that we dread hurt and grief? Is it that we shrink from pain and aching? Is it that, somewhere in our subconscious, we believe that if we avoid such stinging injury, it will somehow pass by us? And if it somehow *should* pass by us, would we be the better or worse for it?

Kahlil Gibran (1883-1931), the Lebanese poet and philosopher, wrote that "Your joy is your sorrow unmasked. And the selfsame well from which your laughter rises was oftentimes filled with your tears." Can we say with Gibran that where there has been no pain, there can be no real joy?

Can we agree with him that the deeper the sorrow carves into our being, the more joy we can contain?

As life's wellsprings continue to pour forth their blessings, we become accustomed to such gain and eventually condition ourselves to believe that we *deserve* such advantage. As time progresses, our familiarity with our gain causes us to take its presence for granted; only when such good suddenly ceases to exist, do we consider our good fortune and realize our richness.

Robert Browning Hamilton, in his following poem titled "Along the Road," eloquently and pointedly expressed the reality of pleasure and pain's benefit to the human spirit:

> I walked a mile with Pleasure;
>
> She chatted all the way,
>
> But left me none the wiser
>
> For all she had to say.

I walked a mile with Sorrow,

And ne'er a word said she:

But, oh, the things I learned from her

When Sorrow walked with me!

Is it not true that, as we travel back through our past, it is during the difficult, trying, and painful times that we learn the true meaning and value of life? Has it not been during these dark hours that we set aright our priorities which have somehow become out of focus or out of order? Is it not during the long nights of tears that we conduct our deepest soul-searching in an attempt to discover *who* and *what* we truly are? Or *who* and *what* we truly **want to become**? Is it not the misery of distress that provides us with the impetus to move forward and overcome existing barriers?

Pearls are never created in a stress-free environment. They are brought forth as the result of a grain of sand entering a shell and causing irritation within that shell. As the living shell responds to the irritation of the foreign invader, the beautiful, opalescent pearl is the result.

Is it not also true that we humans alike must face the bitter and barbed realities of existence so that we may endure and become victorious in the tests of life? As the vine must be pruned to bear greater fruit, so must we be pruned to promote continued growth.

Yet in the midst of our suffering, we often do not desire the keen, finely-honed potential of our being. We would desire, rather, to simply stand on the plateau. But humankind is like the brook's water.

Stopping yields stagnation.

For if we do not move forward in our journey,

we become blunt and dull and unsavory characters.

The Greatest Loss

Death is often expected when one lies bedfast, deteriorating from the effects of old age. Death is expected when one is gravely ill, and all prognoses point to that end. Death is expected when one lives amidst dirt, infestation, and starvation. But the death of a child is never expected. The old, the sick, and the deprived are expected to die.

But never a child.

Not one who is just beginning to live. Not one who has such a short past and such a long, hoped-for future. This isn't supposed to happen. But it does. And sometime it doesn't happen to "other people." Sometimes it happens to US!

Time dictates we will most likely bury our parents. That's the way it's supposed to be. And we realize we stand a fifty percent chance of burying our spouse. That's the way it is in a two-person relationship. But we never envision burying our child. That runs contrary to all the laws of age and order and nature. But sometimes we *do* bury our child, and we must deal with the reality of it all. Our dream of life and love and laughter turns to a nightmare of loss and anguish and tears. Suddenly all the certainties of life turn to questions. Why me? Why my child? How? Did I do something to cause this?

At the moment in history we know our child is dead, it is as though our thoughts and feelings scream to a grinding halt. Nothing moves, yet everything seems to spin into chaos. No thoughts come, yet a multitude of considerations bombard us. Our heart nearly pounds out of our chest, our blood rushes through our veins as if pouring through our skin, and we cease to exist. Yet we continue to live. Attempting to reduce such a moment to words is paramount to reducing the universe to a pin point.

In the moments, hours, days, weeks, and months ahead, we stand in utter shock that the rest of the world continues to function. Our neighbors go on with their lives, our friends' routines continue as before, the stars still sparkle, and "Life Goes On." We don't wish for our loss to be someone else's; we simply don't want it to be *ours*. And we struggle with surviving from day to day.

We don't seem to fit into the present, we yearn for the past, and we temporarily lose hope in the future. We cannot decide if time is our friend or our enemy. We know the initial intensity of the loss will not continue.

It would destroy us.

But we cannot imagine how it will ever be different. It is as though we have been divided in half, with each half trying to find the other.

We oscillate between anger and fear.

Devastation and hope.

Demands and questions.

Those individuals who have been spared this grief can never know the heartache. They may sympathize, but they can never empathize. A child's death is equal to all of nature being thrown into reverse at breakneck speed.

Those of us who have walked this path of grief would like to assist our friends and acquaintances in helping others face this crisis. We have learned from bitter experience what helps and what hurts, and we would like to offer suggestions that will enable you to help someone else who is experiencing such a loss. Perhaps a fitting title would be "Ten Suggestions for Helping a Hurting Parent Survive."

1. **Please don't remind us that we *have*, or *can have*, other children.**
   We realize this, yet no other child can replace our loss. It makes us feel that you are minimizing our loss by suggesting we "add and substitute."

2. **Please don't say it was probably all for the best.**
   Perhaps death *was* for the best, but we desperately want the *best* to be a healthy, living child. It makes us feel that you are being philosophical and impersonal.

3. **Please refer to our child by name.**
   It reminds us that you remember the child . . . not the fact. We need to keep our child personalized. As strange as it may seem, it does bring us comfort to hear that special name.

4. **Please don't ask us how we are doing.**
   We are not *sure* how we are doing. We are not sure of anything at first. We are trying to get back on our feet and find our place in the scheme of things. We know you want us to sound positive and encouraging. But perhaps we just aren't ready for that yet. And questions make us feel very vulnerable.

5. **Please encourage us to talk about our child.**
   Our memories are so vivid, and we want to keep those memories, *and our child,* alive. This talking may bring tears, but those tears can be very therapeutic and are an indispensable aid in the overall healing process. If you have a tender or funny story that involves our child, please share it with us . . . even if we already know it. We want to share memories with the people we know.

6. **Please don't tell us you know how we feel unless you have lost a child.**
It makes us want to scream, "No, you don't! You can't *possibly* know!" We know you want this comment to draw us closer together. But it actually pushes us further away unless you have walked in our shoes and have known the pain we are experiencing.

7. **Please don't ask us if there is anything you can do to help.**
Look at us (and our lives) and *find* a way in which you can help. If nothing else, simply send a card that reminds us you are thinking of us. Or bring us a home-cooked meal, for all daily chores are such a burden at times like these.

8. **Please remember that the first calendar year is especially difficult.**
It is a year of "firsts" for our loss . . . first Christmas, first birthday, first Mother's or Father's Day, etc. Cards and remembrances on special occasions remind us that you, too, are remembering that child we loved.

9. **Please don't be afraid of silence.**
We are not always wanting comforting words, bits of wisdom, or practical suggestions. Sometimes we simply want someone to talk to. And please remember that a physical touch can oftentimes be more comforting than words. A squeeze of the hand, a pat on the shoulder, or a hug can convey many thoughts. They say a picture is worth a thousand words, but so is a physical gesture of compassion.

10. And most importantly of all, please don't avoid us.
Our loss is not contagious, and we need your support.
We know you are uncertain of what to say. So are we.
But allow us to find our way through this experience
together. Please don't stay away, thinking you may
upset us. We have been upset as much as any human
can possibly be, and we will most likely treasure your
presence for a little while.

Our sudden tears may surprise you, and they may make you
feel somewhat uncomfortable. But please remember that such
intense emotions must be released, or they will literally kill us! If
you allow us to experience this phase of the recovery process,
you will be helping us to readjust to life. We don't know how
long the tears will continue.

It may be weeks.

It may be months.

Or even years.

Different individuals heal at different rates and in different
ways. Although we cannot give you a time frame, our bodies and
our spirits will know when it is time to move on.

Then . . . and *only* then . . . can we do so!

And please don't be fearful that you will say something to
remind us of our child. Our loss is uppermost in our minds, but
we will be able to get on with the healing process more quickly if
you simply be *yourself* . . . and allow us to be *ourselves.*

That Final Gift

My husband and I have a good friend named Larry Kniss who has a good father named Al. Or rather *had* a good father named Al.

Al was buried today, and as I attended his funeral, many thoughts came to mind. The usual customs were followed, and the customary words were spoken by family and friends. But much more than that occurred. A *lifetime* of memories were recalled by his family, I'm sure. And those of us who knew him were also recalling our own experiences with him. I had the privilege of knowing this fine gentleman for 32 years, and I never once saw him or spoke to him that he wasn't friendly and pleasant. He held true to form and continued in his congenial manner when I last saw him just four weeks ago.

Al was the president of a machine company that has become internationally known for manufacturing parts and rebuilding machinery used in specific industries. Yet Al never forgot his humble beginnings, his friends, or his appreciation for life. Every Sunday for 15 years, my family knew we would always see this kind gentleman and his wife sitting in their usual place in church. If they were not there, they were either out of town, or one of them was ill.

But Al did not only *attend* church; he *supported* it with his financial resources, his work, and his prayers. He had a wonderful voice, and he used that voice to sing songs from his heart to praise his God and to encourage his fellow worshippers.

Although Al had been in failing health for some time, he continued to anticipate the completion of his lakeshore cabin. He watched vigilantly as each phase of the construction led into the next. He had the pleasure of enjoying his new cabin for a full month before he passed away.

The landscapers were busily putting the finishing touches to the property on that particular day. As the workers were preparing to leave, they parted with, "Goodbye, Mr. Kniss. See you tomorrow."

Al responded, "I'll be here if I'm not in Heaven." Now that was not something that Al said on a regular basis. In fact, his family cannot recall him *ever* saying that before.

He went into his cabin, sat in his favorite chair, and stepped into eternity within fifteen minutes. Did Al have a premonition of what was about to occur? Did he sense that his earthly life was finished and that he was about to make a wonderful transition to a higher level of existence?

Al not only had the admiration of his friends and acquaintances, he had the admiration of his business associates within his plant. They affectionately called him Big Al, and they all seemed to feel that he was their friend as well as their company president. His associates felt that way about him, I believe, because that was the example he set before *them*. In speaking with Al and his two sons who have recently been managing the company, I have never heard them say *I* and *they* when referring to their employees. It has always been *we*. Both father and sons seemed to realize that their success depended upon the *relationships* within that company . . . they were in the endeavor together . . . and what affected one, affected all.

Al's special kind of respect for his associates was revealed today as the pastor read the hand written message that accompanied the basket of flowers from the company:

> In memory of a truly good, caring, and giving man.
> Al was respected and admired by all who knew
> him. He had a positive effect on many lives. It
> was an honor to have known such a man. We will
> miss his cheerful personality. Our condolences to

all of Al's family and to all of those who loved him.

From all of his friends at Scheu and Kniss.

Al started at entry level of the work force many years ago and worked his way through levels of responsibility and skill. That experience caused him to truly *know* the company and appreciate its operations. But as he frequently passed through the plant, calling individuals by name, one could almost forget that he was the CEO. He carried the title, but he did not flaunt it. After all, these were his friends. That bond of professional friendship and consideration was evident at today's service as many of the plant's associates were visibly moved by their loss.

We observe today's business world and wonder what caused us to come to this "dog-eat-dog" working environment where workers constantly fear for their job security, never feel the familiarity of being personally known or appreciated, always must watch their backs for a surprise attack from the rear, and then cannot understand why they do not experience the satisfaction of a job well done as they hear their parents and grandparents speak of. In my conversations with Al and his sons concerning their business, never have I heard them speak in a belittling fashion of *any* of their working associates. Perhaps words of concern over a particular situation, but never comments that would cause hurt or embarrassment to their associates. And in return, never have I heard the associates speak negatively of their top management. It is a true example of "what *goes* around, *comes* around."

And is it not that way with all relationships?

Do we not get from a relationship that which we put into it? Where have we developed the concept of continually *taking* from others, yet never *giving* in return?

And is it not that way in nature?

Do we not continually take from the earth's goodness, yet wonder why natural resources are being depleted at an alarming rate? Do we not go into nature to enjoy its beauty, yet leave behind our garbage of candy wrappers, soft drink cans, and general trash?

There must be cooperation between human and nature if we are to survive.

Oh, yes, Al left his family and friends with one last surprise gift at today's service. He sang at his own funeral!

From a tape made many years ago, he sang from his heart to praise his God and to encourage his fellow man!

Come to think of it, it is not accurate to say Al's wife *had* a good husband and his sons *had* a good father. Perhaps it is a matter of semantics, but it would seem that his wife still *has* a good husband, and his sons still *have* a good father, for he continues to live in their hearts by way of his instructions and his example and his love. As a living man, woman, or child, we always leave a legacy to those who know us. Only *we* can determine what that legacy will be. *We* make that final choice, and *we* leave that final gift!

. . . about

FAITH and
INSPIRATION

"I need not shout my faith. The hills are
mute; yet how they speak of God!"

- Towne

Easter's Victory

There are many customs in many lands that have been developed over the ages to celebrate the Spring Solstice. Different groups of people refer to the celebrations by many names, but the underlying theme is the same throughout the world when various cultures celebrate Easter. That theme is "rebirth and rejuvenation."

The French refer to the season as "Pacques," derived from *pasch,* which literally means "He passes over" (referring to the Jewish Passover). According to Scripture, this was the time God rescued Jews who spread blood over their doorposts. From what were they rescued? From their lives of misery and torture and death and slavery in ancient Egypt.

Christians around the world celebrate Easter on the first Sunday after the first full moon following the first day of Spring in the Northern Hemisphere. During this sacred religious holiday, Christians will take time to reflect upon the true meaning of Easter; it is a time that celebrates the resurrection of Jesus Christ, God's only begotten Son. According to Christian beliefs, it is because of this resurrection that humankind can have the assurance of a Heavenly eternal home through the acceptance of salvation that was provided by way of the shed blood of Calvary. In both Judaism and Christendom, the central theme of Easter is DELIVERANCE and RESCUE.

Many visual symbols are associated with Easter. An empty cross reminds Christians that the resurrected and living Christ is their eternal hope. The display of white Easter Lilies is a reminder of Christ's life of purity. Candles represent Jesus as being the "Light of the World." And the lamb? This lowly and quiet animal, known for its obedience to its shepherd, again represents the life of Christ as He obediently followed the will of His Heavenly Father.

In addition to perhaps buying new spring wardrobe items, coloring eggs, and purchasing baskets of candy goodies, Christians reflect upon the significance of their willingness to become obedient to a higher calling than that of serving their own desires and interests. They contemplate all the events of Holy Week as they consider the days of torment that Christ endured . . . from being falsely accused by His fellow man to experiencing the glorious resurrection from a borrowed tomb.

During the difficult days of Holy Week, Christ was ordered to stand trial before Pontius Pilate (the man who saw no wrong in the life of Jesus, yet permitted His crucifixion because of peer pressure). He was scourged (a debacle that occurred on a knee-high post while the victim was beaten with strands of leather into which were attached bits of stone and broken pottery). Such an inhumane experience often caused the victim to lose his mental faculties as he endured the beating's agony. This was followed by a mandatory carrying of His own heavy cross through the streets of Jerusalem as He struggled toward Calvary's hill. Imagine, if you can, the jeers and taunts of the crowds as He made His way through their midst. And imagine the agony of His followers as they witnessed this horrid trauma their Friend was enduring. The sense of hopelessness they must have felt!

At the appointed place on Calvary's hill, other experiences awaited Christ. He was stripped of His clothing. His hands and feet were nailed to the cross. He was given vinegar to drink. He had a sword thrust into His side. He was mocked and ridiculed. And He endured a death that was reserved for the vilest of criminals.

Being crucified was privately torturous and publicly humiliating. The Roman officials in charge of the crucifixion death were experts in their field, and they prolonged the victim's suffering as long as humanly possible. Crucifixion was an excruciating and agonizing death caused primarily from suffocation rather than blood loss (as many people suppose).

There are written records indicating that victims could live as long as *nine days* on a cross! The pain, the thirst, the torment of daily heat, the hunger, the sense of separation, and the desire simply to die and end the suffering . . . each had to be intense beyond our imagination. All of this agony in the name of love . . . the love of God through His beloved Son Jesus Christ!

As pointed out in the poem titled "One Solitary Life" (author unknown), this Man of Galilee had His beginnings in the most humble of circumstances, never owned a business or real estate, never wrote a bestselling publication, never traveled far from home, and never told people what they wanted to hear. He told them what they *needed* to hear. He spoke to them of truth . . . not fantasy. Yet His life changed the course of history and an eternal destination for millions of people around the world. One Life . . . yet consider what it accomplished.

In his work titled "Easter Tidings," J. Harold Gwynne reminds us of the many blessings of Easter when he writes the following:

> Easter is a Miracle . . .
>   the miracle of newness of life.
>
> Easter is a Glory . . .
>   the glory of resurrection power.
>
> Easter is a Triumph . . .
>   the triumph of love over hate.
>
> Easter is a Promise . . .
>   the promise of unending fellowship.

Easter is a Victory . . .
    the victory of life and death.

Easter is a Hope . . .
    the hope of eternal life.

Scientists tell us that words (sound waves) never die . . . that they are merely absorbed into the world around them. They also inform us that they are attempting to create equipment which will someday be able to extract these sound waves from our universe. What would we hear if we were to place that equipment in Pontius Pilate's courtroom or along the streets of Jerusalem or on Calvary's hill?

What would we hear if such equipment were located in all the places we have visited the last 24 hours, or the last 30 days? Would the world hear words of encouragement, faith, support, and pleasantness? Or would the world hear us complain, criticize, and condemn? If given the opportunity to decide, would we permit the world to listen to our words?

There is obvious power in the *SPOKEN* word, but there is equal power in the *WRITTEN* word. Many years ago I was mourning the death of my best friend . . . my mother. I was thumbing through the pages of an old copy of Easter Ideals magazine and was overjoyed to find one of her published poems from several years before. It reminded me of the power of the pen *and* of the many places where we can find God.

Know That I am God

I am the river, but ye hear me not;
Have ye more faith than the wife of Lot?

I am the sunset at the close of day:
I am the Truth, the Life, and the Way.

I am the snow on the mountain peak.
I am the Bread of Life that ye seek.
I am the air that ye breathe with ease;
I am the bloom on the cherry trees.

I am the river, the brook, and the spring;
But ye hear me not for the world's mad ring.

I am a poem, a prayer, and a song;
I am the light of the world at dawn.

I am the Lilies on Easter Morn;
I am the breath of the newly born.
I am the flowers, the trees, and the sod;
Be ye still . . . and know that I am God.

- Chleo D. Goodman

Take time during the Easter season to contemplate, to dream, and to envision. Set aside time to consider not only the temporal . . . but the eternal!

And if it is *not* Easter, do it anyway. You will benefit and be blessed.

Who Is He . . . Really?

I have often passed individuals like him before . . . many times . . . in different areas of the city, on different days of the week, and in all seasons. I have seen big ones, little ones, young ones, old ones. But they have never captured more than a few moments of my thinking time before. I gave more thought to them during the Christmas season as I dropped my contribution into the round red kettle. But, somehow, during the remainder of the year, they seemed to escape my attention.

Although I was driving down the road, and this man was walking along the sidewalk, his presence seemed to step in front of me. Webster defines him as "a destitute person, without a home or regular job, and rejected by society; abandoned or forsaken." As children, we referred to them by such slang terms as *tramps, vagabonds, hobos*, and *beggars*. But as adults, we attempt to show some dignity to them by saying they are *derelicts* or *homeless people*.

As I drove past this thin, dirty, unshaven man of average height, I could not help but notice his shirt that was far too large as it hung from his frame. His pants were also too large at the waist, and the only reason they did not fall from his body was the fact that they were held in place by a tattered old belt. In addition to being too large, the pants were also too short . . . they showed his bare legs at the ankle and revealed that he wore no socks. His shoes were old and worn, and I'm not sure they even had shoelaces.

His shoulder-length hair was dirty and messy, and it seemed that it had not encountered a brush or a comb for a long time. But as I looked at his hair, I noticed something more disturbing. Beneath that hair was a head that bowed toward the ground, watching the passing concrete as it vanished beneath his feet. And his shoulders . . . stooped and bent as though they had carried the weight of the world upon them.

But in his hand was perhaps the most tragic aspect of his existence . . . a paper bag wrapped and twisted to fit the shape of a whiskey bottle. What did that bottle say? Was it the *cause* of his condition, or was the *effect* of his situation?

I could not help but ask myself how long it had been since his teeth had been brushed or his nails had seen a file. How long had it been since his face felt a razor against it, or his body enjoyed a warm shower? Could he remember his last experience with receiving medical care?

How long had it been since he had eaten? And *what* had he eaten? Had it been a decent meal provided by a mission organization or sympathetic passerby, or had it been junk food (along with his whiskey)? And what about his next meal? Or did he even think of such things? Is he so conditioned to eating only when he stumbles upon food that he does not attempt to plan ahead? Has he found that such planning is futile and only intensifies his hunger?

I wondered what he might be thinking as he walked along that road. Was he pondering how he had arrived at such an existence? Was it something he had endured his entire life, or had something occurred later in life that caused it? Had he suffered a job failure or a family loss? Or had he gambled away his financial reserves?

If he has living family members, have they abandoned him or written him off in disgrace? Do they know his whereabouts? Does he know where *they* are? Do they keep in contact with one another, or will one die without the knowledge of the other? If death occurs, will there even be *concern*? How does one contact a homeless individual such as this?

Does he think of his **past,** or does he deliberately block it from his memory? Are his yesterdays so filled with darkness and the struggle for survival that he simply sees them with a neutral sense of sheer existence? Perhaps he doesn't remember . . . perhaps he doesn't care. If such is the case, can we begin to comprehend the sadness of such a life?

Does he think of his **present,** or is he able to survive only by *not* thinking? Does he notice people's sideways glance as they pass near him? Does he notice their attempt to pretend he doesn't exist? Does it hurt him? Or has he lost his ability to feel emotions? Does one *ever* arrive at that point? If so . . . does that signal the passing from human to machine?

Does he think of his **future,** or does he deliberately block that from his mind also? Are his tomorrows so filled with hopelessness and despair that he simply sees them as something to be endured? As something to be tolerated only when they arrive?

What does he think about as holidays approach? Does his mind go back to days of family and gatherings and food? Or has it been so long since he had family associations that holiday memories are becoming blurred in his mind? Perhaps he is so caught up in the struggle for survival that some holidays slip up on him without notice. Does he even know what day of the week it is?

Does he feel that death would be a welcome visitor that could deliver him from his life of embarrassment and deprivation? Does his existence sometimes seem so futile that he considers taking his own life? Or is the instinct for survival so intense that he wills to keep trudging on?

If he *is* attempting to change his lifestyle, is there someone in his world to encourage him and support him in his efforts? Or are there those around him who do not *want* his change, for it would mean their losing a comrade?

Possibly he may never have heard the word *self-respect,* or he may not know its meaning. But whether or not he recognizes the word, how does he see himself or feel about himself?

Is he content with his life, having perhaps known nothing else?

Does he hate himself, having perhaps known a better period of life during which he knew success?

He obviously has a name. I wonder what it is? How long has it been since he has heard it? Do his street friends know his full name, or just his first name? Or has he changed his name in an attempt to obliterate his real identity?

Or does he care? Perhaps he has known such degradation and humiliation that he is able to block out all else except the passing concrete as it vanishes beneath his feet. Or do we attempt to make *ourselves* feel better by trying to convince our spirits that he does not care?

But that whiskey bottle being carried with such determination . . . what is its real story? And what could it tell us about the man carrying it?

I Saw Him Again

I encountered another of the so-called homeless people today. At least he *looked like* a homeless individual. I had passed him earlier as I was driving to the grocery store, and his image had continued to invade my thoughts. I wondered if he and the other man I saw last week knew each other. Had their paths ever crossed? And if they ever were to meet, would they speak or have any type of conversation? What do homeless people do when they meet each other for the first time? Do they introduce themselves? Do they share some form of street sign language? Or do they tend to ignore one another, as *we* tend to ignore *them*?

It was a rather warm day, yet he wore a long overcoat and hat. He had that same unkempt look that most homeless men have as he walked along the side of the road. He was an older man whose shoulders were stooped and whose walk was slow. Did his appearance portray his true age, or had he been made old before his time due to his lifestyle? Had he ever known a different level of existence, or had this always been his lot in life?

I had noticed that he was carrying what appeared to be a shaped tote bag of some sort, and from the way it easily swung in the air, I assumed it was empty. It reminded me of a diaper bag, but it was a nasty brown, and I couldn't imagine a man in his situation carrying a diaper bag. But I found myself wondering what had been in that bag, or what was *going to be* in it.

I proceeded to the grocery store, caught up in my world of fresh fruits and vegetables, the weekly meat specials, and a written reminder (otherwise known as a grocery list) of other necessary items. I had just completed my trip down aisle 5 when I rounded the corner into aisle 6.

Hmmm . . . that raises an interesting point. Is it possible to *round* a *corner*?

My mind was focused upon getting through aisle 6 and locating those Chinese noodles I needed for my evening meal. My mind was racing among a dozen thoughts. But in the morning's rush, I had forgotten about *him*.

Suddenly we stood face to face at the end of the aisle . . . I with my basket full of goodies, and he with the few items in his tote bag. I looked into his face and saw the creases, saw the lines carved deep by both neglect and the elements of nature.

And in that split second of time, I saw much more. I saw a man whose life was marked by embarrassment and humiliation and deprivation. I saw a man who had been the object of jokes and crude comments. I saw a man who most likely lived in isolation as those around him cut a wide path as they passed by. I saw a man to whom no one spoke, for they knew not what to say.

He may not have been someone's husband or brother or father. But he *was* someone's son. At some point in past history, he had arrived into this world, perhaps surrounded by the hopes and dreams that all parents have for their children as they make their earthly appearance.

And in that same split second of time, I decided.

Perhaps he would never remember my gesture.

Perhaps I was doing it as much for myself as for him.

I paused momentarily, made eye contact with him, and greeted him.

"Good morning, sir. And how are you today?"

I stopped and waited for a response, rather than scurrying by. Would I receive a response? Would I be rebuffed? Would I be ignored?

Suddenly I felt as though I were standing in *his* shoes, having acknowledged my presence to another human being and wondering if I would be acknowledged in return.

It was an uncomfortable sensation, and I suddenly realized that he had most likely endured this awkward sensation many times in his life.

He turned toward me, apparently checking to see if someone had truly spoken to him. Perhaps it had been so many years that he no longer expected acknowledgment or recognition.

He stopped. He returned my smile.

I believe I saw a smile in his eyes, as well. And what a wonderful surprise!

His weathered, dirty hand tipped his worn, misshapen hat in my direction . . . with all the ceremony and finesse that one would expect from the finest English gentleman. He replied, "Just fine, young lady. And how are you today?"

I gave him my usual cheery response for such a beautiful day. "I'm as fine as frog's hair. It's such a wonderful day!"

He seemed to glow. "It certainly is!"

We parted with each of us wishing the other a pleasant day.

As I returned home to the love and security of my family, I found myself wondering where *he* went? Would he eat his food in the same manner as he was buying it . . . alone?

I'm still wondering where he is.

I'm still wondering if he is alone.

Blessings from Unexpected Places

The story is told of three horsemen riding through the desert one night. They came to a dry riverbed and were startled to hear a voice from the darkness warning, "Halt!"

The men obeyed the command, and the voice continued, "You have done as I commanded. Now get off your horses, pick up a handful of pebbles, put them in your pockets, remount your horses, and continue on your journey." Then the voice continued, "Since you have done as I commanded, you will be both glad and sorry that you obeyed me."

The horsemen did not understand what had happened, but they rode on through the night. In the early light of the morning, the riders reached into their pockets and discovered that a miracle had taken place. The pebbles in their pockets had been transformed into magnificently beautiful diamonds, emeralds, rubies, sapphires, and other precious stones.

They remembered the warning . . . that they would be both glad and sorry. They were truly glad they had taken the pebbles.

And truly sorry they had not taken more.

Why did the travelers not take *more* pebbles? Was it because they were told to do so and resented having to do something they perhaps did not *want* to do?

Was it because they did not understand the full meaning behind the command and therefore were not willing to give their full cooperation?

Was it because they felt inconvenienced by having their time intruded upon and resented such an invasion of their lives?

Whatever the reason, we can be sure of one fact. All the horsemen, although grateful for the pebbles they had taken, regretted not having taken more. For had they taken more, they would have increased their wealth. They would have enjoyed the beauty and the bounty of untold blessings.

But who would have anticipated the pebbles turning to gems? How could they have known?

But is life not like that, also? Do we not miss many blessings that could be ours because they come from unexpected places?

Perhaps a business colleague or a friend or a loved one, through a poor choice of words, *tells* us to do something . . . rather than *asks* us. And we, in our childish defiance, balk at the request. Not because it is so outrageous or unreasonable or impractical. But because the proper words or phrases were not spoken. It is a classic case of throwing the baby out with the bath water.

We cannot differentiate between the fact and the phrase, and therefore we refuse both. For the want of a proper word, a blessing was missed. Perhaps we missed the enjoyment of a task well done or the thrill of a project completed.

Perhaps a request is made of us and we do not understand the underlying reasons behind the request. Usually we either insist upon knowing the **5 W's** (who, what, where, when, and why) of the situation, or we do not want to be involved in the matter. How many modern-day conveniences we would be living without if the inventors would have insisted upon knowing all the facts *before* their accomplishments were complete!

Perhaps a request is made, and we find its timing to be extremely poor. We have been leading a fast-paced life recently, and we are feeling the physical fatigue. Or we are under professional pressure, and our stress level has been elevated. Or the children have been giving us fits, and we simply want to be left along. And then someone comes along with a request. And we graciously (or *not* so graciously, perhaps) decline their request.

Could we have missed the untold blessing of knowing that we helped another individual in need, or the blessing of being part of another's accomplishments who only needed help in achieving them?

Could we have missed the indescribable pleasure of watching our children discover new and fascinating things in the world around them because we were too tired or busy with our own interests? Or missed the enjoyable trip down memory lane as we busily pushed aside the elderly ones in our life because we were too busy to take that stroll with them?

We must always remember that we must have a part in the *work* if we want a part in the *blessing*.

We must not only count our BLESSINGS,

but we must consider their SOURCE.

Our pebbles can become precious stones to us, also.

... about

MISCELLANEOUS

"A wise man will make more
opportunities than he finds."

- *Bacon*

Today's Working Woman

Today's workplace is a different sector of society than it has been in the past. It is strenuous by virtue of a downsized workforce, resulting in increased responsibilities, changing job descriptions, and widespread economic uncertainty. The job situation is stressful for idealistic young adults entering the work place, men who have known past job security, and women. But perhaps the greatest weight of pressure is experienced by today's working woman.

Whether married or single, today's working woman is expected to be SuperWoman who feels compelled to simultaneously coordinate domestic responsibilities, professional duties, and personal needs and desires. In this struggle to be "all things to all people," working women are experiencing an intense source of frustration. As working women from recent years continue to stay in unsuitable or insignificant professions of their past, they are growing intensely dissatisfied.

This dissatisfaction is carrying over into the women's professional *and* personal lives, affecting all individuals with whom they come in contact. As with all long term stress, performance suffers in all areas. As the performance level decreases and the dissatisfaction mounts, many women are perceived as unsuitable workforce members who should stay home with children and family *or* recognize their emotional natures and leave the business world in pursuit of personal aspirations within a more domestic framework.

It is at this point that the Catch 22 situation develops. The working woman who feels dissatisfied will experience decreased energy, stamina, and creativity . . . which thereby produces *more* strain . . . which yields even greater decreased energy, stamina, and creativity. The vicious cycle has begun, and no direction but

"DOWN" will be achieved. The elevator is descending, and the basement is the final destination.

But as with many disasters, human intervention can sometimes change the course of events. As with most types of intervention, the necessary steps of change will not be easy, and they may not come as quickly as we would desire. But if this cycle is to be broken, today's unfulfilled working woman must develop a plan to change her future employment situation if she is to become the complete person she envisions.

This author has recently achieved the metamorphosis from discontented and ungratified classroom teacher to happy and fulfilled business/industry/education seminar consultant and trainer . . . and writer. Seventeen years of accumulated classroom frustration prompted me to act upon hidden dreams. I have always enjoyed the teaching procedure and taking part in the learning process, so the desire for some type of continued instruction was my focus.

My desire to be associated with business persons began surfacing more intently, but it was the casual comment from my friend Paula Foster who was aware of my unhappiness that propelled me into action. No divine voices or heavenly trumpets sounded when this comment was made, yet in looking back over the past year, it was at that moment in time that my life took a definite turn toward a more complete and satisfying future.

It takes a great deal of courage to change one's vocational direction, especially after many years in a particular field. But this must be the first step . . . to be willing and determined to take that first step of change. It will most likely cause a few sleepless nights and occasional doubts along the way. But there is no course around this obstacle.

After the decision has been made, take off-work hours to pursue conversations with persons working in, or associated with, your desired field of endeavor. Compile a list of relevant questions and continue asking those questions from various individuals so that comparison of answers will be possible. Begin lifting the ceiling of limitations off yourself as you begin thinking in a more spontaneous and creative way. Breaking old thought and speech patterns is difficult, but it is eased by the desire to begin again.

Seek membership in local civic and business organizations so that you may begin networking with other professionals in your intended field. This process takes time (as does all base-building procedures), but it can become extremely enjoyable as you realize you are discussing matters of personal liking. Do not view these contact persons as someone you can "use." In contrast, communicate with these individuals in a win-win relationship whereby both you and they will benefit from the association.

Become involved in available seminars or with experienced business persons who can teach you the basic principles of starting a business or changing a career. Do not let unforeseen obstacles throw you off course as you continue your endeavor. A *down* day is usually followed by a brighter tomorrow. And remember that you are pursuing your dreams . . . and dreams do not just happen.

If it is financially feasible, it is easier to shift your train of thought if the old vocation can be left behind as you pursue your new career. But if that is not possible, it is also very possible and productive to pursue the *new* as you continue in the *old* until transition is possible.

February is National Heart Month. If you are reading this during February, your timing is perfect! It is an appropriate time to begin being good to your heart, your family and friends, and your whole self to leave that work situation that is holding you back. If it is *not* February, designate this month as your own *personal* National Heart Month. Accept this as the time you choose to turn yourself in a new direction . . . a direction that will bring satisfaction and fulfillment to you!

Downsizing, Upscaling, and Midstreaming

Today's work world offers opportunities and adversities, services and difficulties, values and anxieties. History teaches us that the work environment has constantly undergone change since its inception, but today's changes are occurring so rapidly that many employees are finding themselves reeling from downsized workforce numbers, upscaled responsibilities created by the downsizing, and midstreaming duties that are being reassigned.

Members of the nonmanagement staff have traditionally been referred to as *employees*. However, a recent change in terminology regards them as *associates*, along with other terms of recognition utilized by various companies. But whatever we call them, they are the basis for the continued success of any business endeavor. Conversely, they may also be the cause of failure. But for the purpose of positive focus and guidance, we shall look at today's business world and attempt to offer help to those associates who are struggling with their current, changing work conditions. We will hopefully help them overcome their resistance to change.

But that which can be applied to the American workforce may also be applied in our personal lives as well. Basic fundamental patterns of behavior can be adapted to fit any particular situation, so we may benefit in more than one area of our lives. Such versatile application of information makes our time invested in learning even more valuable.

First, we must recognize the fact that people *are* capable of change. Naturally, that change comes more easily for some individuals than it does for others, but all of us are capable of making that change with the proper instruction and motivation. However, in recognizing this *changing* ability, we must also realize that people cannot be forced to change. They must have a part in deciding whether or not they *will* change. They must also have a part in deciding *how* they will make the change. Associates must realize that, although it would be nice for everyone to have the freedom to do as they chose, the result would be corporate chaos and stagnation as each element of the work force attempted to progress in a different manner and at a different pace.

Change does bring anxiety, but that anxiety can be lessened if one is aware of the steps involved in such a process. First, we must recognize the necessity of releasing old patterns of thought and behavior before change can take place. One might call it the *unfreezing* phase that precedes change.

After we have allowed past patterns to relinquish some of their hold on us, we have permitted ourselves to move into the second phase, or *neutral* stage, of willingness to adapt to new behavior.

Finally, we enter the third phase, or *refreezing* stage, of change which involves the acceptance and application of *new* modes of behavior. We must be willing to explore options during this time, eliminating those which do not suit us . . . and accepting those we find agreeable. At first, these new behaviors may feel strange. But as time progresses, we will realize that our new behaviors seems more comfortable. And we may be surprised to sense that our old behaviors now seem strange, as they have become part of our past.

Needless to say, this is not a once-in-a-lifetime process, but rather a repeated process that will continue throughout our lives as we progress from one level of behavior to another.

As this change process advances, an identity crisis may arise during which we experience self doubt as our new behavior patterns become more prevalent. If we are moving in our desired direction, we must accept the *new self* that emerges. If we have been persistent, in spite of a prolonged identity crisis, and if we have kept practicing the attitudes and behaviors that are associated with our changed self, we will see that our mistakes are decreasing as we continue in the process. After all, we are in a continual learning experience, and everyone makes mistakes during such situations.

Also, as our mistakes become less frequent, we will notice that our apprehension and uncertainty of the change process disappears as we feel more comfortable with our new self. And as that occurs, we will more easily become the person we have been attempting to become during this time. In addition, we will realize that, as our new identity becomes more familiar to us, our old identity seems rather strange, and we no longer feel comfortable with it.

As we succeed in our change process, our self respect increases, and we are able to accept our own worth and shed those self-doubting attitudes that so frequently hold us back in our efforts to achieve our goals. We enjoy the pleasure of seeing our accomplishments, and we realize that we are continuing to grow and learn. And that makes us appreciate ourselves. There is an old adage that tell us, "You can't teach an old dog new tricks." But that is a lie. You *can* teach an older dog new behaviors. And we, as intelligent human beings, *can* learn new behaviors if we have the desire and motivation to do so.

We need to remember that the Chinese word for *crisis* comes from two characters that mean **danger** and **opportunity.** As we face change, it is perfectly normal to feel the anxiety of a *dangerous* situation. But we will also enjoy the satisfaction of having taken control of the opportunity to become that which we desire.

And that is worth feeling good about!

We, the Consumers

Why do many of us,, as consumers, continue to be the gullible recipients of advertising propaganda? The advertising industry systematically and methodically plans its strategy in understanding ideas as to what makes consumers *respond to*, and *purchase*, products. Rather than promoting the products themselves, the industry concentrates upon stimulating human instincts that lie so deeply in the subconscious mind, most consumers are unaware of them.

Advertisers are not addressing "real" needs, but rather needs that are "created" by the industry itself. They study human behavior sufficiently to know that the vast majority of consumers will respond to several persuasive techniques. Most members of the buying public are prime candidates for product consumption when propositioned with the advertising pitch that "This will make me more appealing," "This will raise my status level," "This will add a new dimension to my life," or "I am worth it."

The prime function of advertising is *not* to show a product's true worth, but to create a buying trend. In other words, we (as consumers) are daily *programmed* to think as the advertising industry *wants* us to think, and we are made to feel **inadequate,** thereby responding to products. But the question still remains as to how intelligent, reasoning consumers can be caught in this professional trap?

As we look back over the many decades, we obviously see that each generation has made its own fashion statement and has emphasized its material goods. The 1950s popularized the poodle skirts, the '60s focused on bell-bottomed pants and the mini skirt, and the '70s produced the leisure suit. The '80s brought in the punk rock look with studs, chains, and designer clothes. As we find ourselves in the '90s, we are seeing the retrospective look, with aspects of different time periods being brought into focus together.

But prior to today's emphasis on material prosperity, parents also taught their children the intrinsic value of life, and that view carried them through adulthood. These members of society knew that their value lay in what they *were* rather than what they *did* or *had*. Therefore, they did not rely so heavily upon products that were designed for ego inflation, whether physically, socially, or otherwise.

But our society has changed, and now the value is placed upon a person's attributes, contributions, and possessions. People no longer feel secure within themselves, and they are searching for anything and everything that will help to build them up, both in their own eyes and in the eyes of those around them.

Members of all generations have had their desire for the "in" fashion of the day, but not until recent years have we seen children and young people being murdered for such materialistic items as particular brands of shoes or jackets. We see members of our "civilized" society literally killing one another for articles of clothing!

Narcissism rules where self-love dominates. And excessive interests in one's own appearance, comfort, importance, and abilities reign supreme.

Since most of us firmly believe that people do not have it within themselves to feel content with possessions alone, this advertising/buying cycle will surely continue. People will attempt to find satisfaction and peace by buying "bigger" and "better."

Unless there can be a miraculous turnaround in individuals' value systems, the advertising industry and the marketplace will get richer and richer as they employ more scientific and attractive means of promotion. Meanwhile, we (the consumers) will get poorer and poorer as we continually struggle against our deeply rooted dissatisfaction, believing the advertising propaganda that the purchase of a particular product will bring us more happiness.

Most of us believe that the end product of such thinking

is the empty SELF . . . waiting to be filled with **things.**

We must take the time to sort out our priorities. We must differentiate between our material possessions being important to us, and allowing those very possessions to become our masters. Andrew Carnegie, the Scottish-born American steel manufacturer, was one of the wealthiest individuals of his time. Until his death in 1919, Carnegie was well-known for using his huge fortune to establish many educational, scientific, and cultural institutions.

But on a more personal note, Carnegie proved his mastery over his possessions by a most unusual practice. Each year at Christmas, he would give one of his most treasured possessions to someone as a gift. By doing this, he constantly reminded himself that he was his possessions' master . . . not their slave.

If we, as consumers, are not certain as to where our real values lie, perhaps we could be confronted with the following two questions that would serve as a "sorting out" process:

1. If our home, containing our family members and all our possessions, were engulfed in flames, where would our rescue attempts be directed?

2. If we knew that we were spending our last day on Earth, how would we utilize our time?

In either situation, the advertising industry would likely attempt to convince us, in a subtle manner of course, that we would be wise to also save our stereo or our automobile or our microwave or whatever it is they promote. They would also most likely attempt to convince us that we should enjoy our last hours shopping 'til we drop.

Or would they?

If either incident were to occur, would the members of the advertising world finally be honest with themselves (and with us) and admit that the material things of the world rust and decay and burn . . . that the most important things in life are non-materialistic?

Or have the members of the advertising world *already* been honest with themselves, knowing full-well that their products or services will not create a massive turnaround in our happiness level? Do they continue in their endeavors simply to continue commerce and increase revenue?

We cannot answer for the advertising world.

We cannot answer for others.

But we *can* answer for ourselves!

And we must!

We must . . . if we are to know who we really are.

Birds without Wings

(Written at 29,000 feet somewhere between Atlanta and Louisville.)

We look to the heavens and watch the graceful flight of our fine feathered friends as they gracefully travel from their point of departure to their point of arrival. We watch their apparently effortless gliding as they seem to sometimes float through their journey. Yet underlying that apparent effortless gliding, there are principles of flight and laws of physics in operation. Should any of those principles be disregarded, catastrophic results would occur, and our feathered friends would incur personal injury and perhaps death. Our friends may not personally have realized the existing rules and regulations, but they apply to their survival nonetheless.

We, as humans, also gracefully make our way through life at times, and our endeavors most likely seem to be effortless as others witness our commitment. Only *we* know the true efforts that we put forth.

Our feathered friends utilize the same two eyes for vision whether ground-bound or airborne. Yet those eyes receive such differing perspectives . . . ground-oriented vs. air-oriented. While on the ground, they see only those elements and incidents immediately surrounding them. Yet airborne, they are capable of viewing their world from long distance angles while watching concurrently happening events. They are aware of their own existence while, simultaneously, watching the lives of others. And they realize that what seems to be large and overwhelming from the ground suddenly appears to be small and perhaps even insignificant from the air.

We, as humans, also have limited and distorted vision of our immediately surrounding circumstances. It is only *if* and *when* we are able to stand back that we are able to see our situation as it truly is.

As longer migrations approach, our friends' instincts take control as to time, condition, and location. They do not read a calendar, watch a clock, or check for gas mileage. Their internal, unseen instinct shifts into overdrive as they progress toward their desired destination. Yet sometimes there is a glitch in our friends' navigational system, and they veer off course. Perhaps the cause of such veering is illness, injury, or carelessness attention to details. The veering may not be intentional, yet the consequences are the same. *Intent does not always equal results.* Perhaps the cause is a change in the familiar landmarks. But whatever the cause of the off-course flight, our feathered friends successfully navigate the majority of the time, even during the course of landmark changes. Their navigational system rarely fails them.

We, as humans, often seem to possess an inner sense of direction and discernment as we travel through life. Our "sixth sense" detects things we would otherwise miss. Yet sometimes, due to circumstances, we are not in tune with that extra sense of perception, and we miss the mark. The cause for such error may be due to various elements. But whether our veering off course is intentional or not, we often suffer undesirable consequences.

Externally, our friends are recognized by their feathery wardrobe or "signature." Red for cardinals. Blue for jays. Yellow for finches. Gray for doves. Etcetera. Their colors and patterns specify their type. And their type regulates their behavior. But their behavior may be altered by circumstances or instruction. Birds have also been responsible for man's signature, as man wrote many early words with the quill pen. Recycling from one species to another.

We, as humans, often judge others by their outward appearance. And if there is something we see that is different about them, we ostracize them or keep them at a distance. We expect certain behavior from prescribed appearances and clothing.

We are alerted to our feathered friends' pleasant presence by their joyful singing as they soak up the world around them. In return, they contribute to nature with their uplifting melodies. Conversely, we are acquainted with their frightening or angry predicaments by their squawking or screeching.

We, as humans, frequently transmit our thought patterns or inner health by our chipper comments and smiling faces. Conversely, we show our *down* side by complaints, criticisms, and downcast glances.

Our feathery friends' family structure is emphasized as expectant mothers meticulously prepare nests for soon-to-arrive young, and fathers assist in their youngsters' upbringing. Both parents work together for the benefit of their offspring. And when one parent is missing, the burden for the remaining parent is several-fold. Birds of the same species usually find camaraderie among their peers, and they will join together in warding off strangers. The incoming birds may not pose a real threat, but their differing appearance signals stress and fear. The distinct message is . . . *Difference = Difficulty!*

We, as humans, also have nesting instincts that enable us to prepare for the coming of our own offspring. We often join together in fellowship among ourselves but quickly push away those whom we feel do not qualify

for presence within our group. We do not stop to consider that difference *could* represent welcome variety.

As our fine feathered friends begin their lift-off, that sinking feeling occurs at the moment in time before there is sufficient wind under their wings to support the upcoming journey. But as their speed and altitude increase, those laws of flight and physics again take control. The point of arrival becomes a closer reality.

We, as humans, also experience that sinking sensation shortly after beginning a new endeavor. It usually lasts until we build up enough *steam* to get the proverbial ball rolling and get on with our responsibility.

However, with all their natural instincts and learned behaviors, we must accept the fact that sometimes our feathered friends get themselves into predicaments from which they cannot free themselves. One such example is the duck who remains in freezing water until he suddenly finds himself frozen into it. Due to his down and bodily oils, he will not usually die from hypothermia. He may starve to death, but he will not die from loss of heat under normal circumstances. But the cause of his death is merely an academic matter, for death is death . . . whether from lack of food or lack of warmth.

We, as humans, also get ourselves into difficulties from which we find it extremely difficult to escape. Sometimes we sit so long in the status quo that when we realize the danger in which we have placed ourselves, it is too late to correct the problem; we suffer painful ramifications as the result of our actions.

But in spite of all the aspects of bird behavior discussed, the final, *and most important,* element of our friends' existence is TEAMWORK. It is through this unified effort that all members of the flock benefit.

We, as humans, also must come to the realization that we must work together in order for success to be realized. No man or woman is an island, and we do not stand alone. We were not created to live in isolation and, therefore, we must be willing to allow our grief or joy, and bounty or poverty, to be shared by those around us.

On a printed sheet many years ago, I read the following (source and author unknown):

FIVE LESSONS OF THE GEESE

Have you ever wondered why geese fly in a "V" formation? There is a reason why they do, and there are many lessons we can learn from their seemingly unusual behaviors.

Researchers have learned that as each bird flaps its wings, it creates an uplift for the bird immediately following. The "V" formation is estimated to add 70% to the flock's flying range.

Lesson #1: *Those who share a common direction and sense of community can get where they are going more quickly and easily because they travel on the thrust of another's efforts.*

Whenever a goose moves out of formation, it feels the drag and air resistance of trying to go it alone. It quickly gets back into formation to take advantage of the lifting power of the bird immediately in front.

Lesson #2: *If we have as much sense as a goose, we will stay in formation when headed in the same direction.*

	When the head goose gets tired, it rotates back in the wing, and another flies point.
Lesson #3:	*Take turns on hard jobs.*

The geese honk from behind to encourage those in front to keep up their speed.

Lesson #4:   *We need to be careful of what we say when we honk from behind.*

When a goose gets sick or is wounded by gunfire and falls, two geese drop out of formation and follow it down to provide help and protection. They stay with it until it is either able to fly or is dead, then set out to catch up with their flock, flying on their own or with another flock.

Lesson #5:   *Stand by one another.*

End of Lesson

At the end of my flight into Louisville, I was able to steal a few moments of time from our "lead bird," Captain Wayne Stradley (whom I learned was a Louisville native). I asked him what special responsibilities that he, as our plane's captain, faced each time he carried a load of passengers to their intended destination. He responded that he felt a strong paternalistic outlook, considering that his passengers had entrusted their lives into his keeping. He went on to elaborate that he was ever-vigilant in observing preflight checks, weather patterns, airport conditions, possible technical difficulties, the location of other aircraft, and any other circumstances that might be hazardous to his crew and passengers. The captain also commented that he felt his overall responsibility was to ensure a good work and flying environment for all concerned.

But Captain Stradley took on a most human quality as he stated, "Before we take off, I picture my grandmother sitting in the cabin. I not only want her to arrive safely, but I want her enjoy her trip with a sense of security, peace of mind, and enjoyment."

I liked his idea.

I think I will fly with Captain Stradley as often as possible, being one of his "Birds without Wings."

Man vs. Animal

The term *animal-world* is used by many authors to refer to a situation in which each species has a **fixed** relationship to the surrounding environment, although there may be individual differences among members of each species. Considering that species' structures are predetermined by biological equipment, and that the species are often geographically restricted, it is referred to as a "closed" world.

This concept is in opposition to the "open" world of the *man-world* wherein man is found over a larger area of the planet's surface, not being biologically restricted by geography. Yet given these two basic differences, one must recognize the positive and negative aspects of belonging to the man-world.

Both man and beast have proven that they are capable of adjusting to environmental variances, although some changes obviously require a longer adjustment period than others.

Among animals, there is a definite social order, and each animal knows its place. This pecking order is oftentimes decided by size or strength or aggression. Such animal hierarchy was witnessed in our home several years ago as my daughter bred and raised guinea pigs to sell in an attempt to raise her share of the purchase price of her desired horse. We were not aware of it transpiring at the time, but one day we suddenly noticed that Blondie seemed to go where she pleased and do as she pleased, with the other females staying out of her way. Second, third, and fourth places were also established, with the fourth-ranking female taking whatever the other three females "dished out."

The only event that altered the social order was the removal or death of one of the animals. And I must admit that we were surprised to find such a structured situation among such low-order animals as guinea pigs! Needless to say, humans also establish the pecking order based upon beauty, intelligence, power, fame, and other pertinent factors relating to the individual situation. One might refer to these criteria as *swords of judgment.*

With animals, sick and dying members of the community are often left to die alone, being shunned by the other members. With the exception of family members and close friends, this is often true with humans, as they seem to be very uncomfortable with the dying process. Of course, human emotions come into play in a situation such as this that are not readily observed in the animal kingdom. Crippled or deformed animals are often neglected, apparently with the notion that they cannot carry their own weight within the community. Unfortunately, we humans also respond similarly to disabled members of **our** communities.

There do appear to be bonds of affection and protection within closely knit animal groups, such as there are within human groups. And in both cases, although there may be friction and fighting among the members themselves, they will join together in times of stress and danger to protect themselves from the enemy. One major difference in this area of conflict is that animals do not appear to carry resentment against their own members for social code violations as do humans.

Another visible similarity within both animal and human social groups is external behavior of the members. In both cases, those members who exhibit *unusual* or *other-than-expected* behavior patterns do not receive the same response from the community as do those members whose behavior is synonymous with other members' behavior. The major difference in the community's response is that of **type.** Whereas animals tend to ostracize and run off unruly members by means of *biting,* humans do so by means of *ignoring.*

So perhaps man and beast are not so different!

As to which is better, it would depend upon whether one would choose to go through life meeting the demands and satisfactions on a daily basis with no regard to future reimbursement. Or whether one would choose to accept the frustrations and hardships and pain incurred in being a human. If one is concerned with having the ability to think, feel, analyze, synthesize, and contribute to the future - - - the choice is simple.

HOMO SAPIENS is the way to go.

Or is it? Perhaps we have many questions to which only the animals have the answers!

Dear Reader:

I've Been Thinking ... about Living, Loving, and Learning was conceived in my mind in the summer of '96. But you have helped give it life by giving of yourself. You have given your time, your energy, and your thoughts as you traveled through its pages.

My purpose in writing this book was to allow you, the reader, the opportunity to stop and appreciate the world around you, to consider the events of everyday life, and to ponder the circumstances in which you find yourself.

Has *I've Been Thinking ... about Living, Loving, and Learning* affected you in any particular way? Has it made a difference in your life? If so, will you please take a few moments and write to me? Please share your thoughts with me so that I can become better acquainted with you. Please include your full name, address, and complete phone number. Some of these responses may be shared in future editions, and I must be able to contact you for permission to use your reply.

Send all correspondence to:

Alpha Publishing
A division of Alpha Consulting
c/o Carol G. Heizer
P.O. Box 18433
Louisville, KY 40261-0433

And have a good day!

YES, I want "**I've Been Thinking . . . about Living, Loving, and Learning**" by *Carol Goodman Heizer*.

Send me _____ copies at $12.95 each, plus $3 shipping per book. (Kentucky residents please include $.80 state sales tax per book.) Allow 4-6 weeks for delivery.

Name _____

Address _____

_____

City _____ State _____

Zip _____ - _____

Phone (_____) _____ - _____

Make check payable and return to:

Alpha Publishing, A division of Alpha Consulting
P.O. Box 18433
Louisville, KY 40261-0433
(502) 239-0761
FAX (502) 239-0764